ALLERGY-FREE
COOKBOOK

D0579368

Publications International, Ltd.

Louis Weber, CEO
Publications International, Ltd.
7373 North Cicero Avenue
Lincolnwood, IL 60712

Photography on pages 4, 7 and 9 copyright © Shutterstock, Media Bakery and Jupiter Images.

Recipe development on pages 26, 44, 65 and 122 by Carissa Kinyon.

Recipe development on pages 27, 34, 38, 43, 46, 48, 56, 70, 82, 84, 86, 90, 95, 106, 108, 109 and 134 by Marilyn Pocius.

Photography on pages 35, 39, 45, 49, 57, 83, 87, 107 and 123 by Chris Cassidy Photography, Inc.
Photographer: Chris Cassidy
Photographer's Assistant: Daniel Green
Prop Stylist: Nancy Cassidy
Food Stylists: Vanessa Dubiel, Carol Smoler
Assistant Food Stylist: Mitch Naparalla

Pictured on the front cover *(clockwise from top right):* Basic Oatmeal Cookies *(page 100),* Chicken Saltimbocca *(page 68),* Magic Rainbow Pops *(page 80)* and Turkey and Winter Squash Tacos *(page 54).*
Pictured on the back cover *(top to bottom):* Whole Wheat Brownies *(page 104)* and Basil Chicken with Rice Noodles *(page 56).*

Contributing Writer: Marilyn Pocius

ISBN-13: 978-1-60553-071-0
ISBN-10: 1-60553-071-9

Library of Congress Control Number: 2009936103

Manufactured in China.

8 7 6 5 4 3 2 1

Note: This book is for informational purposes and is not intended to provide medical advice. Neither Publications International, Ltd., nor the authors, editors or publisher takes responsibility for any possible consequences from any treatment, procedure, exercise, dietary modification, action, or applications of medication or preparation by any person reading or following the information in this cookbook. The publication of this book does not constitute the practice of medicine, and this cookbook does not replace your physician, pharmacist or health-care specialist. **Before undertaking any course of treatment or nutritional plan, the authors, editors and publisher advise the reader to check with a physician or other health-care provider.**

Not all recipes in this cookbook are appropriate for all people with food allergies or sensitivities. Health-care providers and registered dietitians can help design specific meal plans tailored to individual needs.

Publications International, Ltd.

table of contents

p. 120

Introduction

Recipes

the basics of allergy-free cooking

What Is a Food Allergy?

The term "food allergy" means different things to different people. It can be a life threatening condition, a mild sensitivity to a particular ingredient, or anything in between. By definition, a true allergy is one in which the body's immune system overreacts to a protein that is normally harmless. Symptoms can range from a rash to anaphylactic shock. Milk, egg and nut allergies are classic examples.

Food sensitivities or intolerances are often also called allergies, though they don't fit the same narrow definition. For example, many people are sensitive to the lactose in milk products and have trouble digesting it. Strictly speaking, they are lactose intolerant, not allergic to dairy. Those with celiac disease have an autoimmune condition caused by a reaction to the gluten in food. It is a serious, chronic condition, not a true allergy. Others choose to avoid certain foods because they feel better physically or mentally when they abstain.

Always have your doctor evaluate your allergies. Misinterpreting symptoms or self-diagnosing can be dangerous.

You Are Not Alone

It is estimated that more than 11 million people have food allergies and the number appears to be growing. According to the Centers for Disease Control and Prevention, the number of children allergic to foods has increased 18% in the last decade. There are many theories, but no proven explanations for  this increase. The good news is that a great deal of research is underway and awareness of the problem has increased everywhere from the classroom to the doctor's office.

Eating Well Without

Dietary restrictions can be an opportunity as well as a burden. Try new ethnic ingredients such as rice noodles or nutritious grains like quinoa. You'll find ideas to inspire you and recipes to delight you right here.

THE EIGHT MOST COMMON FOOD ALLERGENS

In 2004, the FDA identified eight foods that represent 90% of food allergies. By law, they must be listed on food labels.

Milk

Tree nuts

Eggs

Peanuts

Wheat

Fish

Shellfish

Soybeans

Note: *This book does not specifically label recipes that are free of fish, shellfish or soy products, though many recipes included do not contain these allergens.*

The Icons and Their Meaning

 Recipes with this icon are gluten-free as well as wheat-free.

 Recipes with this icon are dairy-free (no milk, cheese, yogurt or other dairy).

 Recipes with this icon contain no eggs or egg products.

 Recipes with this icon contain no tree nuts or peanuts.

Variations to the recipes are given when appropriate. For instance, if cheese or other dairy products can be eliminated, a dairy-free option is included under the main recipe with the appropriate icons.

how to go gluten-free and love it

What Is Gluten Anyway?

Gluten is a protein that is found naturally in wheat, rye and barley. It is the same protein that provides structure for most baked goods. When yeast or baking powder produces gas that causes a loaf of bread or a cake to rise, the stretchy strands of gluten expand and provide structure.

Celiac Disease versus Gluten Sensitivity

There are many reasons people choose to avoid gluten. Celiac disease is the most serious. In the 1% of Americans diagnosed with this autoimmune disorder, exposure to even small amounts of gluten can cause intestinal damage and result in symptoms from fatigue and depression to anemia and bone disease. It is estimated that thousands more might have undiagnosed celiac disease, as many as one out of every 133. If you suspect you may be one of them, it is important to see your doctor for a test before you start eating gluten-free. Many other people just feel better when they avoid gluten, and a smaller number are allergic to wheat itself.

No More Bread? No Pasta?

At first going gluten-free may sound awfully limiting. Fortunately, there are many more delicious foods on the gluten-free list than the forbidden list. There are also more and more products, from cereals to baking mixes to pastas, which are now being formulated in gluten-free versions. These days you'll find them not just in health food stores and on websites, but also on the shelves of most major supermarkets.

The Good News

Since 2004, the FDA's Food Allergy Labeling Law has required that any product containing wheat or derived from it must say so on the label. This means that many ingredients that used to be questionable, such as modified food starch and maltodextrin, must now show wheat as part of their name if they were made from it. Be aware that this ONLY applies to foods produced in the U.S. and Canada.

Just Say No (contain gluten): barley, beer, blue cheese, bulgur, cereal, commercial baked goods, couscous, durum, graham, gravies and sauces, imitation seafood, malt, malt flavoring and malt vinegar, oats, pizza, pretzels, rye, seitan, semolina, spelt, wheat

Maybe: (check the ingredients): flavoring and fillers, frozen vegetables with sauces or seasoning, marinades, mustards, salad dressings, soups, soy sauce

Say Yes (have no gluten): beans, buckwheat, cellophane noodles, chickpea flour, cornmeal, corn grits, fresh fruits and vegetables, lentils, meat and poultry, millet, nuts, potatoes, quinoa, rice, rice noodles, seafood, soy, tapioca, tofu

the gluten-free pantry

Cooking gluten-free is easier if you keep these staples on hand.

❑ all-purpose flour blend, gluten-free

❑ beans and lentils

❑ cereal, gluten-free corn and rice

❑ chickpea (garbanzo) flour

❑ cornstarch and cornmeal

❑ corn tortillas and taco shells

❑ pasta, gluten-free

❑ polenta

❑ quinoa

❑ rice, wild rice, arborio rice

❑ rice flour (brown, white and sweet rice flour)

❑ rice noodles

❑ tapioca flour (also called tapioca starch)

❑ xanthan gum

cooking dairy-free and easy

Two Kinds of Sensitivity

1. Lactose Intolerance

Lactose is the natural sugar in milk. Many people don't produce enough of an enzyme (lactase) to properly digest lactose. When they drink milk, they experience symptoms like stomach pain or diarrhea. If you are lactose-intolerant, you may be able to enjoy some dairy. Cheese and butter tend to be lower in lactose than milk. This is because they contain less milk sugar (but more fat). You are the best judge of what works for you.

2. Milk Allergy

As with other true allergies, being allergic to milk means that your immune system overreacts to a protein—usually casein or whey in this case. Symptoms of a milk allergy can be mild or as severe and life-threatening as anaphylactic shock. If you have a true milk allergy, it's important to avoid all dairy in any form.

Be a Label Detective

Did you know that most margarine contains dairy? Are you aware that hydrolyzed casein and whey powder are dairy products? Fortunately, U.S. food manufacturers are now required to list the simple word "milk" as

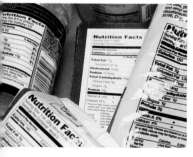

part of the ingredient list or in boldface type at the end of the list, even if the actual ingredient goes by an obscure chemical name. The recent popularity of the vegan diet is a boon for the dairy-free shopper, too. Since vegans consume no animal products, you can assume products labeled vegan are dairy-free. The kosher designation "pareve" is another handy indicator that the product contains no milk.

Celebrate the Naturally Dairy-Free

It's more fun to find new things you CAN eat than to concentrate on the forbidden. Asian cuisines tend to be mostly dairy-free. Japanese sushi, teriyaki and noodle dishes are perfect examples. Chinese menus offer plenty of ideas, too. Most stir-fries, noodle dishes and sauces contain no dairy. And many of them are also gluten-free! Using coconut milk as they do in Thai dishes is a wonderful way to enjoy the rich creaminess missing from some dairy-free cooking.

You Won't Miss the Moo

Going dairy-free might be one of the healthiest things you can do for your diet. You'll be eating less animal fat and probably fewer calories. With a bit of planning and the recipes in this book, dairy-free meals can be easy, nutritious and delicious.

Non-Dairy is NOT always Dairy-Free

Many products labeled non-dairy contain whey, casein or other milk-derived ingredients. According to the FDA, non-dairy products can contain 0.5% or less of milk products by weight. Non-dairy creamers and non-dairy whipped toppings usually contain dairy in some form.

the dairy-free pantry

Cooking dairy-free is easier if you keep these staples on hand:

- ☐ cheese alternatives
  (read labels carefully)
- ☐ cocoa powder, unsweetened
- ☐ coconut butter or oil
- ☐ coconut milk, unsweetened
- ☐ dairy-free margarine
  (read labels carefully)
- ☐ dairy-free semisweet
  chocolate and chips
  (read labels carefully)

- ☐ nutritional yeast
- ☐ soy creamer
- ☐ soymilk, rice milk,
  almond milk, oat milk
- ☐ tofu, silken and regular
- ☐ vegan mayonnaise
- ☐ vegetable shortening

egg allergies, unscrambled

Egg allergies usually occur in early childhood and more than half of those are outgrown by age seven. Of course, as with all allergies, there are exceptions. In some cases, the allergy remains lifelong or first surfaces in adolescence or adulthood. Both the yolk and the white of an egg contain proteins that can cause a reaction.

An Egg by Any Other Name

At first blush, avoiding eggs sounds simple. Just don't eat them poached, scrambled, fried or over easy! Unfortunately, eggs are present in many foods and hide under many names. Most baked goods use eggs for richness and lightness and the shiny crust on breads and pastries is created with an egg wash. Commercially made pancakes, waffles, donuts, crackers and pretzels usually contain eggs, as do many sauces and prepared entrées. Chances are most food that is battered or breaded also contains egg, since it helps the coating stick. Pasta and noodles are usually made with eggs, but there are some egg-free versions available.

Label Lingo

You probably know that you must avoid mayonnaise, meringue and custard. You may not know that there are some obscure ingredient names that are aliases for eggs. Any word beginning with the prefix "ovo" is suspicious. Albumin and globulin are also egg products. Always read labels carefully and check for the allergen statement, which legally must appear somewhere.

Baking without Cracking an Egg

In many baked goods requiring no more than three eggs, silken tofu is an acceptable replacement. (Use ¼ cup of tofu to replace each egg.) One mashed banana or ¼ cup of applesauce can often fill in for one egg in quick breads or muffins that are on the sweet side.

When Is an Egg Substitute NOT a Substitute?

Most cholesterol-free egg substitutes are made from egg whites. They were created to allow people to enjoy eggs without the cholesterol found in the yolks. There are a few egg-free replacement products, but check labels carefully. Look for one that specifies "vegan."

nut allergies in a nutshell

Tree Nuts and Peanuts

Both tree nuts and peanuts are considered together in this book, and recipes free from both are marked with the nut-free icon. You are probably aware that peanuts are legumes, not nuts. You may also know that many children and adults who are allergic to peanuts are also allergic to tree nuts and vice versa.

It's Nuts Not to Be Cautious

While very few reactions are severe, even a mild allergic response to nuts should be taken seriously. Future reactions can be more troublesome. Peanut allergy is responsible for more fatalities than any other food allergy. Even trace amounts can cause reactions.

Tree nuts include almonds, Brazil nuts, cashews, filberts (hazelnuts), macadamia nuts, pecans, pine nuts (pignoli), pistachios and walnuts. A person may be allergic to only one or two tree nuts, but it's best to avoid them all unless you are certain.

A Nut by Any Other Name

Nut proteins can be present in candies, cookies, crackers and other processed foods. Peanut oil is frequently used for cooking, especially in Asian and other ethnic recipes. Read labels carefully every time. Don't assume that ingredients haven't changed—they often do.

When Is a Nut Not a Nut?

When it's a water chestnut or a nutmeg. Neither is botanically related to tree nuts or peanuts, so they rarely present a problem. Coconut is a fruit and is usually not allergenic. However, the FDA recently reclassified it as a tree nut, so products that contain coconut now carry a warning. Pine nuts are also considered tree nuts, but are sometimes tolerated. Soy nuts are legumes, not nuts. Consult your doctor and when in doubt, don't!

Some Nutty Substitutions

Nuts used as a topping can easily be replaced with crushed potato chips, corn chips or toasted bread crumbs. Sunflower or pumpkin seeds can be excellent nut replacements, if they are tolerated. Sunflower seed butter or soy nut butter can stand in for peanut butter.

better breakfasts

ham and potato pancakes

gluten-free | dairy-free | nut-free

¾ pound Yukon gold potatoes, peeled, grated and squeezed dry (about 2 cups)

¼ cup finely chopped green onions

2 eggs, beaten

1 cup (4 to 5 ounces) finely chopped cooked ham

¼ cup rice flour

¼ teaspoon salt

¼ teaspoon black pepper

2 to 3 tablespoons vegetable oil

Chili sauce or mild fruit chutney (optional)

1. Combine grated potatoes, green onions and eggs in large bowl; mix well. Add ham, rice flour, salt and pepper; mix well.

2. Heat 2 tablespoons oil in large heavy skillet. Drop batter by heaping tablespoonfuls and press with back of spoon to flatten. Cook over medium-high heat 2 to 3 minutes per side. Remove to paper towels to drain. Add remaining 1 tablespoon oil, if necessary, to cook remaining batter. Serve pancakes with chili sauce.

Makes 4 servings (4 pancakes each)

breakfast rice pudding

gluten-free | dairy-free | egg-free | nut-free

2 cups vanilla soymilk, divided

¾ cup uncooked whole grain brown rice*

⅓ cup packed light brown sugar

½ teaspoon salt

½ teaspoon ground cinnamon

¼ cup golden raisins or dried cranberries

½ teaspoon vanilla

Mixed berries (optional)

Check cooking time on package. Some brown rice may require a slightly longer cooking time.

1. Bring 1½ cups soymilk to a boil in medium saucepan. Stir in rice, brown sugar, salt and cinnamon. Return to a boil. Reduce heat; cover and simmer 15 minutes.

2. Stir in remaining ½ cup soymilk and raisins. Cover; simmer 10 to 15 minutes or until rice is tender. Remove from heat; stir in vanilla. Serve with berries, if desired.   **Makes 4 servings**

note: Rice thickens as it cools. For a thinner consistency, stir in additional soymilk just before serving.

TIP Rice for breakfast is traditional in most Asian cultures and makes a great start to anyone's day. Brown rice is more nutritious and flavorful than ordinary white rice, though it does take longer to cook. When you're preparing rice, make a big batch. You can easily freeze leftover cooked rice for later use. After it cools in the refrigerator, pack 1- or 2-cup portions in resealable freezer bags. Press out as much air as possible, label and freeze them. Rice thaws easily in the microwave or a steamer.

summer fruit brunch cake

gluten-free | dairy-free | nut-free

¾ cup gluten-free all-purpose flour blend

½ cup cornmeal

1 teaspoon xanthan gum

½ teaspoon baking powder

¼ teaspoon baking soda

½ cup (1 stick) dairy-free margarine, softened

⅔ cup granulated sugar

2 eggs

½ cup vanilla soy yogurt

1 cup fresh peach slices *or* 1 can (about 15 ounces) sliced peaches in juice, drained

Sliced strawberries

Additional vanilla soy yogurt

1. Preheat oven to 325°F. Spray 9-inch pie plate with nonstick cooking spray. Combine flour, cornmeal, xanthan gum, baking powder and baking soda in medium bowl.

2. Beat margarine and sugar in large bowl with electric mixer at medium speed until fluffy. Add eggs and ½ cup yogurt; beat until well combined. Beat in flour mixture until combined. Stir in peaches.

3. Pour batter into prepared pie plate. Bake 35 minutes or until toothpick inserted into center comes out clean. Top with strawberries and drizzle with yogurt.

Makes 6 servings

ham and asparagus quiche

 gluten-free | nut-free

2 cups sliced asparagus (½-inch pieces)
1 red bell pepper, diced
1 cup milk
2 tablespoons rice flour
3 eggs
1 cup chopped cooked deli ham
2 tablespoons chopped fresh tarragon or basil
½ teaspoon salt
¼ teaspoon black pepper
½ cup (2 ounces) finely shredded Swiss cheese

1. Preheat oven to 350°F. Combine asparagus, bell pepper and 1 tablespoon water in microwavable bowl. Cover with waxed paper; microwave on HIGH 2 minutes or until vegetables are crisp-tender. Drain vegetables.

2. Whisk together milk and rice flour in large bowl. Whisk in eggs until well blended. Stir in vegetables, ham, tarragon, salt and black pepper. Pour into 9-inch pie plate.

3. Bake 35 minutes. Sprinkle cheese over quiche; bake 5 minutes longer or until center is set and cheese is melted. Let stand 5 minutes before serving. Cut into 6 wedges. **Makes 6 servings**

 gluten-free | dairy-free | nut-free

Replace milk with plain soymilk and omit Swiss cheese or use a dairy-free cheese alternative.

blueberry pancakes
with blueberry-spice syrup

 dairy-free | nut-free

   Blueberry-Spice Syrup (recipe follows)
 1 cup all-purpose flour
 2 tablespoons sugar
 2 teaspoons baking powder
¼ teaspoon salt
¾ cup plain or vanilla soymilk
 2 egg whites
 1 tablespoon dairy-free margarine, melted
½ cup blueberries

1. Prepare Blueberry-Spice Syrup; keep warm.

2. Combine flour, sugar, baking powder and salt in medium bowl. Beat soymilk and egg whites in small bowl; stir in margarine. Add soymilk mixture to flour mixture, stirring until almost smooth. Gently fold in blueberries.

3. Coat large nonstick skillet with cooking spray. Heat over medium heat until water droplets sprinkled on skillet bounce off surface. Drop batter by ¼ cupfuls into skillet. Cook 2 to 3 minutes until bubbles appear at edges and bottoms of pancakes are lightly browned. Turn pancakes; cook until bottoms of pancakes are lightly browned. Serve with Blueberry-Spice Syrup.
                                              Makes 4 servings

blueberry-spice syrup

gluten-free | dairy-free | egg-free | nut-free

½ cup blueberries, divided
½ cup maple syrup, divided
½ teaspoon grated lemon peel
½ teaspoon ground cinnamon
¼ teaspoon ground nutmeg

Bring ¼ cup blueberries and ¼ cup syrup to a boil in small saucepan over medium heat. Mash hot berries with fork. Add remaining ¼ cup blueberries and ¼ cup syrup, lemon peel, cinnamon and nutmeg. Cook and stir over medium heat about 2 minutes or until heated through.

Makes 1 cup

veggie-beef hash

gluten-free | dairy-free | nut-free

   Nonstick cooking spray

 4 ounces cooked roast beef, finely chopped

1 ½ cups frozen seasoning blend*

 1 cup shredded potatoes, squeezed dry

 ½ cup shredded carrots

 1 egg

 ½ teaspoon dried rosemary

 ½ teaspoon black pepper

 ½ cup salsa (optional)

Frozen seasoning blend is a combination of finely chopped onion, celery, bell peppers and parsley flakes found in the freezer section of the supermarket. Frozen or fresh sliced bell peppers and onion may be substituted.

1. Combine beef, seasoning blend, potatoes, carrots, egg, rosemary and black pepper in large bowl.

2. Lightly spray large nonstick skillet with cooking spray; heat over medium-high heat. Add beef mixture; press down firmly to form large cake. Cook 4 minutes or until browned on bottom, pressing down on cake several times. Turn. Cook 4 minutes or until lightly browned and heated through. Serve with salsa, if desired.　　　**Makes 2 servings**

TIP Use whatever type of meat you have on hand for a breakfast hash—deli meat, leftover burgers or sausage— almost anything works. For a vegetarian version, add tofu or more vegetables. Hash is an excellent way to turn last night's leftovers into a hot, hearty breakfast.

breakfast pizza

 gluten-free | nut-free

2 cups frozen shredded hash brown potatoes, thawed

½ cup finely chopped onion

¼ cup tomato paste

2 tablespoons water

½ teaspoon dried oregano

2 eggs, scrambled

½ cup (2 ounces) shredded mozzarella cheese

2 tablespoons bacon bits

1. Combine potatoes and onion in medium bowl.

2. Lightly spray medium nonstick skillet with cooking spray. Add potato mixture; flatten with spatula. Cook 7 to 9 minutes per side or until both sides are lightly browned.

3. Mix tomato paste and water in small bowl; spread evenly over potatoes in skillet. Sprinkle with oregano.

4. Pour eggs over mixture. Cover and cook 4 minutes. Sprinkle with cheese and bacon bits. Cover; cook 1 minute.

5. Slide pizza from skillet onto serving plate. Cut into 4 wedges.

Makes 2 to 4 servings

 gluten-free | dairy-free | nut-free

Omit cheese; instead, top with cooked vegetables or a dairy-free cheese alternative.

scrambled tofu and potatoes

 gluten-free | dairy-free | egg-free | nut-free

potatoes

- ¼ cup oil
- 4 to 5 red potatoes, cubed
- ½ white onion, sliced
- 2 tablespoons dairy-free margarine or olive oil
- 1 tablespoon minced fresh rosemary
- 1 teaspoon coarse salt

scrambled tofu

- ¼ cup nutritional yeast
- ½ teaspoon turmeric
- 2 tablespoons water
- 2 tablespoons soy sauce
- 1 package (14 ounces) firm tofu
- 1 tablespoon oil
- ½ cup chopped green bell pepper
- ½ cup chopped red onion
- 2 green onions, chopped

potatoes

1. Preheat oven to 450°F. Place oil in 12-inch cast-iron skillet; place skillet in oven 10 minutes before ready to bake potatoes.

2. Bring large saucepan of water to a boil. Add potatoes; cook 5 to 7 minutes or until tender. Drain and return to saucepan. Stir in onion, margarine, rosemary and salt. Spread mixture in preheated skillet. Bake 25 to 30 minutes or until potatoes are browned, stirring every 10 minutes.

scrambled tofu

3. Combine nutritional yeast and turmeric in small bowl. Stir in water and soy sauce.

4. Cut tofu into 8 cubes. Gently squeeze out water and loosely crumble tofu into medium bowl. Heat 1 tablespoon oil in large skillet over medium-high heat. Add green pepper and red onion; cook and stir 2 minutes or until soft but not browned. Add tofu; drizzle with 3 tablespoons turmeric mixture. Cook and stir about 5 minutes or until liquid is evaporated and tofu is uniformly colored. Stir in additional turmeric mixture, if desired, for stronger flavor.

5. Divide potatoes among 4 serving plates. Top with tofu and sprinkle with green onions.   **Makes 4 servings**

breakfast quinoa

gluten-free | dairy-free | egg-free | nut-free

½ cup quinoa
1 cup water
1 tablespoon packed brown sugar
2 teaspoons maple syrup
½ teaspoon cinnamon
¼ cup golden raisins (optional)
   Sliced strawberries and banana
   Soymilk

1. Place quinoa in fine-mesh strainer; rinse well under cold running water. Transfer to small saucepan. Stir in water, brown sugar, maple syrup and cinnamon. Bring to a boil. Reduce heat; simmer, covered, 10 to 15 minutes or until quinoa is tender and water is absorbed. Add raisins, if desired, for last 5 minutes of cooking time.

2. Top quinoa with strawberries and bananas. Serve with soymilk.
                                                        Makes 2 servings

cornmeal-pecan pancakes

 gluten-free | dairy-free

1 cup yellow cornmeal
¼ cup rice flour
⅓ cup sugar
1 teaspoon baking powder
½ teaspoon baking soda
¼ teaspoon salt
⅛ teaspoon nutmeg
1 cup plain or vanilla soymilk
1 egg
1 tablespoon canola oil
½ teaspoon vanilla
¼ cup chopped pecans
   Nonstick cooking spray
   Maple syrup

1. Combine cornmeal, rice flour, sugar, baking powder, baking soda, salt and nutmeg in large bowl; mix well. Combine soymilk, egg, oil and vanilla in medium bowl; whisk until smooth. Add soymilk mixture to dry ingredients; stir until smooth batter forms. Stir in pecans.

2. Spray griddle or large nonstick skillet with nonstick cooking spray; place over medium-high heat. Spoon 2 tablespoons batter onto hot griddle for each pancake; spread to 3-inch diameter. Cook 2 to 3 minutes or until tops of pancakes are bubbly; turn and cook 1 minute more or until bottoms are lightly browned. Serve with syrup.   **Makes 8 servings**

 gluten-free | dairy-free | nut-free

Omit the chopped pecans or substitute sunflower seeds or other non-allergenic seeds.

breakfast tacos

 gluten-free | nut-free

   6 mini corn taco shells *or* 2 regular-sized corn taco shells
   2 eggs
   Nonstick cooking spray
½ teaspoon gluten-free taco seasoning mix
   2 tablespoons shredded Cheddar cheese
   2 tablespoons mild salsa
   2 tablespoons chopped fresh parsley
   Shredded lettuce

1. Heat taco shells according to package directions; cool slightly. Meanwhile, beat eggs in small bowl until well blended. Spray small skillet with cooking spray; heat over medium-low heat.

2. Pour eggs into skillet; cook and stir until desired doneness. Sprinkle eggs with taco seasoning mix.

3. Spoon egg mixture into taco shells. Top each taco with 1 teaspoon each cheese, salsa and parsley. Add green onion and lettuce, if desired.

Makes 2 servings

 gluten-free | dairy-free | nut-free

Omit the Cheddar cheese or substitute a dairy-free alternative.

lite bites

spanish tortilla

gluten-free | dairy-free | nut-free

1 tablespoon olive oil
1 cup thinly sliced peeled potato
1 small zucchini, thinly sliced
¼ cup chopped onion
1 clove garlic, minced
1 cup shredded cooked chicken
8 eggs
½ teaspoon salt
½ teaspoon black pepper
¼ teaspoon red pepper flakes
    Fresh tomato salsa (optional)

1. Heat oil in 10-inch nonstick skillet over medium-high heat. Add potato, zucchini, onion and garlic; cook and stir about 5 minutes or until potato is tender, turning frequently. Stir in chicken; cook 1 minute.

2. Meanwhile, whisk eggs, salt, black pepper and red pepper flakes in large bowl. Carefully pour egg mixture into skillet. Reduce heat to low. Cover and cook 12 to 15 minutes or until egg mixture is set in center.

3. Loosen edges of tortilla and slide onto large serving platter. Let stand 5 minutes before cutting. Serve with salsa, if desired.

Makes 6 to 8 servings

greek salad
with dairy-free "feta"

gluten-free | dairy-free | egg-free | nut-free

dairy-free "feta"

- 1 package (about 14 ounces) firm or extra-firm tofu
- ½ cup extra virgin olive oil
- ¼ cup lemon juice
- 2 teaspoons salt
- ½ teaspoon black pepper
- 2 teaspoons Greek or Italian seasoning
- 1 teaspoon onion powder
- ½ teaspoon garlic powder

salad

- 1 pint grape tomatoes, halved
- 2 seedless cucumbers, sliced
- 1 yellow bell pepper, cut into slivers
- 1 small red onion, cut into thin slices

1. Cut tofu crosswise into 2 pieces, each about 1 inch thick. Place on cutting board lined with paper towels; top with layer of paper towels. Place weighted baking dish on top of tofu. Let stand 30 minutes to drain. Pat tofu dry and crumble into large bowl.

2. Combine oil, lemon juice, salt, pepper and Greek seasoning in small jar with lid; shake to combine well. Reserve ¼ cup for salad dressing. Add onion powder and garlic powder to remaining mixture. Pour over tofu and toss gently. Refrigerate overnight or for at least 2 hours.

3. Combine tomatoes, cucumbers, bell pepper and onion in serving bowl. Add tofu "feta" and reserved dressing. Toss gently.

Makes 4 to 6 servings

winter squash risotto

gluten-free | egg-free | nut-free

2 tablespoons olive oil

1 small butternut or medium delicata squash, peeled and cut into pieces

1 large shallot or small onion, finely chopped

½ teaspoon paprika

¼ teaspoon salt

¼ teaspoon dried thyme

¼ teaspoon black pepper

1 cup arborio rice

¼ cup dry white wine (optional)

4 to 5 cups hot vegetable broth

½ cup grated Parmesan or Romano cheese

1. Heat oil in large skillet over medium heat. Add squash; cook 3 minutes, stirring frequently. Add shallot; cook 3 to 4 minutes or until squash is almost tender. Stir in paprika, salt, thyme and pepper. Add rice; stir to coat with oil.

2. Add wine, if desired; cook and stir until wine evaporates. Reduce heat to low. Add ½ cup broth; cook over medium heat, stirring occasionally. Stir in another ½ cup broth when almost all liquid is absorbed. Repeat with remaining broth until consistency is creamy and rice is tender. (Total cooking time will be 20 to 30 minutes.)

3. Stir in cheese; season with additional salt and pepper. Serve immediately. Makes 4 to 6 servings

gluten-free | dairy-free | egg-free | nut-free

Omit Parmesan cheese, or replace it with a dairy-free cheese alternative.

sizzling rice flour crêpes

gluten-free | dairy-free | egg-free | nut-free

crêpes
1 cup rice flour

½ teaspoon salt

½ teaspoon sugar

½ teaspoon turmeric

1 cup unsweetened coconut milk

½ to ¾ cup water

filling and garnishes
Vietnamese Dipping Sauce (recipe follows)

½ cup vegetable oil

1 bunch green onions, chopped

1 cup chopped cooked chicken, small raw shrimp or cubed tofu

2 cups bean sprouts

Lettuce, fresh cilantro and fresh mint

1. Combine rice flour, salt, sugar and turmeric in medium bowl. Gradually whisk in coconut milk and ½ cup water until batter is thickness of heavy cream. Let batter rest at least 10 minutes. (Add additional water if needed to thin batter after resting.) Prepare Vietnamese Dipping Sauce.

2. Heat 9- or 10-inch nonstick skillet over medium heat. Add 3 teaspoons oil to skillet. Add ¼ cup filling to skillet (about 1 tablespoon green onion, plus 3 tablespoons chicken, shrimp, tofu or a combination). Cook and stir 2 to 4 minutes or until onions are softened and shrimp is pink and opaque, if using. Pour about ½ cup batter over filling mixture. Immediately swirl to coat skillet and filling with batter.

3. In 30 seconds or when sizzling sound stops, add bean sprouts to 1 side of crêpe. Cover pan and cook 3 minutes or until sprouts wilt and center of crêpe appears cooked. Edges should be browned and crisp.

4. Fold crêpe in half with spatula and transfer to plate. Repeat with remaining batter and fillings.

5. Serve crêpes with lettuce, herbs and Dipping Sauce. Traditionally, crêpes are eaten by wrapping bite-size portions in lettuce with herbs and dipping each bite in sauce. **Makes 4 to 6 servings**

vietnamese dipping sauce: Combine ⅔ cup water, ¼ cup gluten-free soy sauce, 2 tablespoons sugar and juice of 1 lime in a small bowl. Stir until sugar dissolves. Stir in 1 clove minced garlic and 1 minced pepper.

tip: Sizzling Crêpes (Banh Xeo, pronounced bahn SAY-oh) are a popular Vietnamese street snack. The word "Xeo" in Vietnamese mimics the sound the batter makes as it sizzles in the pan. The filling can be almost anything you wish. Try using leftover pork, beef, vegetables or whatever you have on hand.

mediterranean veggie bake

gluten-free | dairy-free | egg-free | nut-free

2 tomatoes, sliced

1 small red onion, sliced

1 medium zucchini, sliced

1 small eggplant, sliced

1 small yellow squash, sliced

1 large portobello mushroom, sliced

2 cloves garlic, minced

3 tablespoons olive oil

2 teaspoons chopped fresh rosemary leaves

⅔ cup dry white wine

Salt and black pepper

1. Preheat oven to 350°F. Grease bottom of oval casserole or 13×9-inch baking dish.

2. Arrange slices of vegetables in rows, alternating different types and overlapping slices to make attractive arrangement; sprinkle evenly with garlic. Combine olive oil and rosemary in small bowl; drizzle over vegetables.

3. Pour wine over vegetables; season with salt and pepper. Cover loosely with foil. Bake 20 minutes. Uncover; bake 10 to 15 minutes or until vegetables are tender. **Makes 4 to 6 servings**

tip: Feel free to use whatever vegetables you have on hand or in your garden.

mini carnitas tacos

gluten-free | egg-free | nut-free

1 ½ pounds boneless pork loin, cut into 1-inch cubes
1 onion, finely chopped
½ cup reduced-sodium chicken broth
1 tablespoon chili powder
2 teaspoons ground cumin
1 teaspoon dried oregano
½ teaspoon minced chipotle chile in adobo sauce
½ cup pico de gallo
2 tablespoons chopped fresh cilantro
½ teaspoon salt
12 (6-inch) corn tortillas
¾ cup (3 ounces) shredded sharp Cheddar cheese
3 tablespoons sour cream

slow cooker directions

1. Combine pork, onion, broth, chili powder, cumin, oregano and chipotle in slow cooker. Cover; cook on LOW 6 hours or on HIGH 3 hours or until pork is very tender. Pour off excess cooking liquid.

2. Shred pork with 2 forks; stir in pico de gallo, cilantro and salt. Cover and keep warm.

3. Cut 3 circles from each tortilla with 2-inch biscuit cutter. Top each with pork, cheese and sour cream.   Makes 12 servings (36 mini tacos)

gluten-free | dairy-free | egg-free | nut-free

Omit the shredded cheese and sour cream or replace them with your favorite dairy-free alternatives.

mushroom gratin

dairy-free | egg-free | nut-free

4 tablespoons dairy-free margarine, divided
1 small onion, minced
8 ounces (about 2½ cups) sliced cremini mushrooms
2 cloves garlic, minced
4 cups cooked elbow macaroni, rotini or other pasta
2 tablespoons all-purpose flour
1 cup plain soymilk
½ teaspoon salt
½ teaspoon black pepper
½ teaspoon dry mustard
½ cup fresh bread crumbs
1 tablespoon extra virgin olive oil

1. Preheat oven to 350°F. Heat 2 tablespoons margarine in large skillet over medium-high heat. Add onion; cook and stir 2 minutes. Add mushrooms and garlic; cook and stir 6 to 8 minutes or until vegetables soften.

2. Melt remaining 2 tablespoons margarine in medium saucepan over low heat. Whisk in flour; cook and stir 2 minutes without browning. Stir in soymilk. Bring to a boil over medium-high heat, whisking constantly. Reduce heat to maintain a simmer. Add salt, pepper and mustard. Whisk 5 to 7 minutes or until sauce thickens. Toss pasta with mushroom mixture in skillet; add sauce. Stir gently to combine.

3. Spoon mixture into shallow baking dish or casserole. Top with bread crumbs and drizzle with olive oil. Cover; bake 15 minutes. Uncover and bake 10 minutes or until bubbly and browned.   **Makes 4 to 6 servings**

quinoa and roasted corn

gluten-free I dairy-free I egg-free I nut-free

1 cup uncooked quinoa

½ teaspoon salt

4 ears corn *or* 2 cups frozen corn

¼ cup plus 1 tablespoon vegetable oil, divided

1 cup chopped green onions, divided

1 teaspoon coarse salt

1 cup quartered grape tomatoes or chopped plum tomatoes, drained*

1 cup cooked black beans, rinsed and drained

¼ teaspoon grated lime peel

Juice of 1 lime (about 2 tablespoons)

¼ teaspoon sugar

¼ teaspoon cumin

¼ teaspoon black pepper

Place tomatoes in fine-mesh strainer and place over bowl 10 to 15 minutes.

1. Place quinoa in fine-mesh strainer; rinse well under cold running water. Transfer to medium saucepan; add 2 cups water and ½ teaspoon salt. Bring to a boil over high heat. Reduce heat; cover and simmer 15 to 18 minutes or until water is absorbed and quinoa is tender. Transfer quinoa to large bowl.

2. Meanwhile, remove husks and silk from corn; cut kernels off cobs. Heat ¼ cup oil in large skillet over medium-high heat. Add corn; cook 10 to 12 minutes or until tender and light brown, stirring occasionally. Stir in ⅔ cup green onions and coarse salt; cook and stir 2 minutes. Add corn to quinoa. Gently stir in tomatoes and black beans.

3. Combine lime peel, lime juice, sugar, cumin and black pepper in small bowl. Whisk in remaining 1 tablespoon oil until blended. Pour over quinoa mixture; toss lightly to coat. Sprinkle with remaining ⅓ cup green onions. Serve warm or chilled.

Makes 6 to 8 servings

socca
(niçoise chickpea pancake)

gluten-free I dairy-free I egg-free I nut-free

    1 cup chickpea flour*
    ¾ teaspoon salt
    ½ teaspoon coarsely ground pepper
    1 cup water
    5 tablespoons olive oil, divided
 1½ teaspoons minced fresh basil or ½ teaspoon dried basil
    1 teaspoon minced fresh rosemary or ¼ teaspoon dried rosemary
    ¼ teaspoon dried thyme

Chickpea flour is also called garbanzo flour. It is found in the specialty food section of most supermarkets.

1. Sift chickpea flour into medium bowl. Stir in salt and pepper. Gradually whisk in water to create a smooth batter. Stir in 2 tablespoons olive oil. Allow batter to rest at least 30 minutes.

2. Preheat oven to 450°F. Place 9- or 10-inch cast iron skillet in oven to heat 10 minutes before ready to bake socca.

3. Add basil, rosemary and thyme to batter; whisk until smooth. Carefully remove skillet from oven using oven mitts. Add 2 tablespoons olive oil to skillet; swirl to coat evenly. Immediately pour in batter.

4. Bake socca 12 to 15 minutes or until edge begins to pull away and center is firm. Remove skillet; turn oven to broil.

5. Brush socca with remaining tablespoon oil and broil 2 to 4 minutes until dark brown in spots. Cut into wedges and serve warm.

Makes 6 servings

tip: Socca are pancakes made of chickpea flour and are commonly served in paper cones as a savory street food in the south of France, especially around Nice. Chickpea flour can also be used to make a thinner batter and cooked in a skillet to make a softer crêpe. Just increase the amount of water in the recipe by about ¼ cup.

sweet potato gnocchi

gluten-free | dairy-free | egg-free | nut-free

1½ pounds sweet potatoes (2 or 3 medium)

¼ cup sweet rice flour,* plus additional for rolling

1 tablespoon lemon juice

1 teaspoon salt

½ teaspoon xanthan gum

½ teaspoon nutmeg

½ teaspoon black pepper

¼ teaspoon sugar

2 to 4 tablespoons extra virgin olive oil

1 pound spinach, thick stems removed

Sweet rice flour is sometimes labeled glutinous rice flour (although it is gluten-free) or mochiko (the Japanese term). It is available in the Asian section of large supermarkets, at Asian grocers and on-line.

1. Preheat oven to 375°F. Poke sweet potatoes with fork in several places; bake 50 to 60 minutes or until very soft. Remove skins; put flesh through ricer or mash very well. Discard skins and stringy pieces. You should have about 2½ cups mashed sweet potato.

2. Place mashed sweet potato in medium bowl. Add rice flour, lemon juice, salt, xanthan gum, nutmeg, pepper and sugar. Mix well.

3. Heavily flour work surface with rice flour. Scoop portions of dough onto surface; roll into ½-inch-thick rope using floured hands. Cut into ¾-inch pieces. Shape each piece into oval; make ridges with tines of fork. Transfer to foil-lined baking sheet. Freeze gnocchi at least 30 minutes on baking sheet.**

4. Heat 1 tablespoon oil in large nonstick skillet. Add gnocchi in batches and cook, turning once, until lightly browned and warmed through adding additional oil as needed to prevent sticking. Keep warm.

5. Add olive oil to coat bottom of skillet. Add spinach; cook and stir 30 seconds or just until barely wilted. Serve gnocchi on bed of spinach.

Makes 4 servings

**Gnocchi may be made ahead to this point and frozen for up to 24 hours. For longer storage, transfer frozen gnocchi to freezer container or freezer food storage bags.*

tuna tabbouleh salad

dairy-free | egg-free | nut-free

1 cup water

¾ cup uncooked fine-grain bulgur wheat

1 teaspoon grated lemon peel

3 tablespoons lemon juice

1 clove garlic, minced

½ teaspoon salt

⅛ teaspoon black pepper

1 tablespoon olive oil

1 cup grape tomatoes, halved

1 cup peeled, seeded and chopped cucumber

¼ cup finely chopped red onion

3 cans (5 ounces each) chunk white tuna packed in water, drained and flaked

½ cup chopped Italian parsley

4 cups watercress, tough stems removed

1. Bring water to a boil in small saucepan. Remove from heat and add bulgur. Cover and let stand 15 minutes. Rinse bulgur in fine-mesh strainer under cold water to cool; drain well.

2. Meanwhile, combine lemon peel, lemon juice, garlic, salt and pepper in large bowl. Slowly whisk in olive oil. Add tomatoes, cucumber, onion and bulgur; stir to combine. Gently stir in tuna and parsley. Arrange watercress on 4 serving plates; spoon about 1½ cups salad onto each plate.   Makes 4 servings

gluten-free | dairy-free | egg-free | nut-free

Omit bulgur wheat. Instead, use 1 cup of quinoa cooked according to package directions.

falafel nuggets

 gluten-free | dairy-free | nut-free

sauce

2½ cups tomato sauce

⅓ cup tomato paste

2 tablespoons lemon juice

2 teaspoons sugar

1 teaspoon onion powder

½ teaspoon salt

falafel

2 cans (15 ounces each) chickpeas, rinsed and drained

½ cup rice flour

½ cup chopped fresh parsley

1 egg

¼ cup minced onion

Juice of 1 lemon

2 tablespoons minced garlic

2 teaspoons ground cumin

½ teaspoon ground red pepper

¼ cup vegetable oil

1. For sauce, combine tomato sauce, tomato paste, lemon juice, sugar, onion powder and salt in medium saucepan. Simmer over medium-low heat 20 minutes; keep warm.

2. Meanwhile, preheat oven to 400°F. Coat baking sheet with nonstick cooking spray.

3. Combine chickpeas, rice flour, parsley, egg, lemon juice, minced onion, garlic, cumin, ½ teaspoon salt and red pepper in food processor or blender. Process until well blended. Shape mixture into 1-inch balls.

4. Heat oil in large nonstick skillet over medium-high heat. Fry falafel in batches until browned. Place 2 inches apart on baking sheet; bake 8 to 10 minutes. Serve with warm sauce. **Makes 12 servings**

tip: Falafel can also be baked completely to reduce fat content. Spray balls lightly with nonstick cooking spray and bake 15 to 20 minutes, turning once.

hearty main dishes

turkey and winter squash tacos

gluten-free | dairy-free | egg-free | nut-free

4 corn taco shells
2 teaspoons vegetable oil
¼ cup finely chopped onion
1 cup diced cooked butternut or delicata squash (see Note)
1 teaspoon gluten-free taco seasoning mix
1 cup chopped cooked turkey, warmed
  Salt and black pepper
¼ cup salsa
1 small avocado, peeled and cut into 8 thin wedges

1. Preheat oven to 325°F. Place taco shells on baking sheet; heat according to package directions.

2. Meanwhile, heat oil in large skillet over medium-high heat. Add onion; cook and stir 3 minutes. Add squash and taco seasoning mix; cook and stir 2 to 3 minutes.

3. To assemble tacos, place ¼ cup turkey in each taco shell. Season with salt and pepper. Top with squash mixture, 1 tablespoon salsa and 2 slices avocado.   **Makes 2 servings**

note: Some supermarkets carry packaged diced squash; simply follow the cooking instructions on the package. To use whole squash, peel the squash, cut in half and remove the seeds. Cut the squash into ¾-inch-long strips, then cut crosswise into ¾-inch chunks. Measure 1 cup squash. Heat 1 tablespoon vegetable oil in a medium skillet. Add the squash; cook and stir over medium-low heat 10 to 15 minutes or until fork-tender.

basil chicken with rice noodles

 gluten-free | dairy-free | egg-free | nut-free

1 pound boneless skinless chicken breasts, cut into bite-size pieces
5 tablespoons gluten-free soy sauce, divided
1 tablespoon white wine or rice wine
3 cloves garlic, minced
1 tablespoon grated fresh ginger
8 ounces (about half a package) rice noodles
1 red onion, sliced
1 yellow or red bell pepper cut into strips
2 medium carrots, cut into matchstick-size pieces
2 jalapeño or serrano peppers,* chopped
Juice of 2 limes
2 tablespoons packed brown sugar
1½ cups loosely packed fresh basil leaves, shredded
1 to 2 tablespoons vegetable oil

Hot peppers can sting and irritate the skin, so wear rubber gloves when handling peppers and do not touch your eyes.

1. Place chicken in shallow dish. Combine 3 tablespoons soy sauce, wine, garlic and ginger in small bowl Pour over chicken and stir to coat. Marinate 30 minutes at room temperature or refrigerate for up to 2 hours.

2. Place noodles in medium bowl. Cover with hot water; let stand 30 minutes or until soft. Drain well.

3. Combine onion, bell pepper, carrots and jalapeño peppers in medium bowl. For sauce, stir together remaining 2 tablespoons soy sauce, lime juice and brown sugar in small bowl.

4. Heat large skillet or wok over medium-high heat. Add oil to coat. Add chicken with marinade; cook and stir until no longer pink. Add vegetables. Stir-fry 4 to 6 minutes or until vegetables begin to soften.

5. Stir sauce to dissolve sugar and add to skillet. Cook and stir 2 minutes. Stir in drained rice noodles and basil. Makes 4 to 6 servings

lentil stew
over couscous

dairy-free | egg-free | nut-free

3 cups dried lentils (1 pound), sorted and rinsed

3 cups water

1 can (about 14 ounces) vegetable broth

1 can (about 14 ounces) diced tomatoes

1 large onion, chopped

1 green bell pepper, chopped

4 stalks celery, chopped

1 medium carrot, sliced

2 cloves garlic, chopped

1 teaspoon dried marjoram

¼ teaspoon black pepper

1 tablespoon olive oil

1 tablespoon cider vinegar

4½ to 5 cups hot cooked couscous

slow cooker directions

1. Combine lentils, water, broth, tomatoes, onion, bell pepper, celery, carrot, garlic, marjoram and black pepper in slow cooker; stir. Cover and cook on LOW 8 to 9 hours or until vegetables are tender.

2. Stir in oil and vinegar. Serve over couscous.   Makes 12 servings

tip: Lentil stew keeps well in the refrigerator for up to 1 week. Stew can also be frozen in an airtight container for up to three months.

gluten-free | dairy-free | egg-free | nut-free

Instead of couscous, serve the stew over cooked quinoa.

pad thai

gluten-free | dairy-free | egg-free

8 ounces (about half a package) uncooked rice noodles

2 tablespoons rice wine vinegar

1½ tablespoons gluten-free fish sauce*

1 to 2 tablespoons fresh lemon juice

1 tablespoon ketchup

2 teaspoons sugar

¼ teaspoon red pepper flakes

1 tablespoon vegetable oil

1 boneless skinless chicken breast (about 4 ounces), chopped

2 green onions, thinly sliced

2 cloves garlic, minced

3 ounces small raw shrimp, peeled

2 cups fresh bean sprouts

¾ cup shredded red cabbage

1 medium carrot, shredded

3 tablespoons minced fresh cilantro

2 tablespoons chopped unsalted dry-roasted peanuts

Lime wedges

Fish sauce is available at most large supermarkets and Asian markets.

1. Place noodles in medium bowl. Cover with hot water; let stand 30 minutes or until soft. Drain well. Combine rice wine vinegar, fish sauce, lemon juice, ketchup, sugar and red pepper flakes in small bowl.

2. Heat oil in wok or large nonstick skillet over medium-high heat. Add chicken, green onions and garlic. Cook and stir until chicken is no longer pink. Stir in noodles; cook 1 minute. Add shrimp; cook about 3 minutes or just until shrimp turn pink and opaque. Stir in fish sauce mixture; toss to coat evenly. Add bean sprouts and cook until heated through, about 2 minutes.

3. Serve with shredded cabbage, carrot, cilantro, peanuts and lime wedges.   **Makes 4 to 6 servings**

 **gluten-free | dairy-free | egg-free | nut-free**

Omit the chopped peanuts and top with sesame seeds instead.

pork curry
over cauliflower couscous

gluten-free | dairy-free | egg-free | nut-free

- 3 tablespoons olive oil, divided
- 2 tablespoons mild curry powder
- 2 teaspoons minced garlic
- 1½ pounds pork (boneless shoulder, loin or chops), cubed
- 1 red or green bell pepper, diced
- 1 tablespoon cider vinegar
- ½ teaspoon salt
- 2 cups water
- 1 large head cauliflower

1. Heat 2 tablespoons oil in large saucepan over medium heat. Add curry powder and garlic; cook and stir 1 to 2 minutes until garlic is golden.

2. Add pork; cook and stir 5 minutes or until pork is browned. Add bell pepper and vinegar; cook and stir 3 minutes or until bell pepper softens. Sprinkle with salt.

3. Add water; bring to a boil. Reduce heat; simmer 30 to 45 minutes, stirring occasionally, until liquid is reduced and pork is tender, adding additional water as needed.

4. Meanwhile, trim and core cauliflower; cut into equal pieces. Place in food processor fitted with metal blade. Process using on/off pulsing action until cauliflower is in small uniform pieces about the size of cooked couscous. Do not purée.

5. Heat remaining 1 tablespoon oil over medium heat in 12-inch nonstick skillet. Add cauliflower; cook and stir 5 minutes or until cooked crisp-tender. *Do not overcook.* Serve pork curry over cauliflower.

Makes 6 servings

roast turkey breast
with sausage and apple stuffing

gluten-free | dairy-free | egg-free

8 ounces bulk pork sausage

1 medium apple, peeled and finely chopped

1 shallot or small onion, finely chopped

1 stalk celery, finely chopped

¼ cup chopped hazelnuts

½ teaspoon rubbed sage, divided

½ teaspoon salt, divided

½ teaspoon black pepper, divided

1 tablespoon butter, softened

1 whole boneless turkey breast (4½ to 5 pounds), thawed if frozen

4 to 6 fresh sage leaves (optional)

1 cup chicken broth

1. Preheat oven to 325°F. Crumble pork sausage into large skillet. Add apple, shallot and celery; cook and stir until sausage is cooked through and apple and vegetables are tender. Stir in hazelnuts, ¼ teaspoon each sage, salt and pepper. Spoon stuffing into shallow roasting pan.

2. Combine butter with remaining ¼ teaspoon each sage, salt and pepper. Spread over turkey breast skin. (If desired, arrange sage leaves under skin.) Place rack on top of stuffing. Place turkey, skin side down, on rack. Pour broth into pan.

3. Roast turkey 45 minutes. Remove turkey from oven; turn skin side up. Baste with broth. Return to oven; roast 1 hour or until meat thermometer registers 165°F. Let turkey rest 10 minutes before carving.

Makes 6 servings

vegan pesto

gluten-free | dairy-free | egg-free

1 cup packed fresh basil leaves
½ cup pine nuts, toasted*
2 cloves garlic
½ teaspoon salt
¼ teaspoon black pepper
¼ cup olive oil

Place pine nuts in small saucepan. Heat over low heat 2 minutes or until light brown and fragrant, shaking occasionally.

1. Place basil, pine nuts, garlic, salt and pepper in food processor; drizzle with 1 tablespoon olive oil. Process about 10 seconds or until coarsely chopped. With motor running, drizzle in remaining olive oil. Process about 30 seconds or until finely chopped.

2. Use immediately or refrigerate in airtight container up to 1 week.

Makes ½ cup pesto

gluten-free | dairy-free | egg-free

"cheesy" vegan pesto: Add ⅓ cup nutritional yeast to food processor with basil and drizzle with an additional tablespoon of olive oil.

TIP Pine nuts are seeds and not, strictly speaking, nuts. If you are allergic to tree nuts it is possible you may be able to tolerate pine nuts, but don't take any chances! Under U.S. labeling law, pine nuts are in the same category as tree nuts. People are seldom allergic to just one type of nut, so it's best to avoid all types when in doubt. See page 11 of the introduction for more information.

sesame ginger-glazed tofu

gluten-free | dairy-free | egg-free | nut-free

1 package (14 ounces) extra firm tofu
1 cup gluten-free sesame ginger stir-fry sauce, divided
1 cup uncooked long grain rice
4 medium carrots, chopped (about 1 cup)
4 ounces snow peas, halved (about 1 cup)

1. Cut tofu crosswise into 2 pieces, each about 1 inch thick. Place on cutting board lined with paper towels; top with layer of paper towels. Place weighted baking dish on top of tofu. Let stand 30 minutes to drain.

2. Spread ½ cup stir-fry sauce in small baking dish. Place tofu in sauce; marinate at room temperature 30 minutes, turning once.

3. Meanwhile, cook rice according to package directions. Keep warm.

4. Spray indoor grill pan with nonstick cooking spray; heat over medium-high heat. Place tofu in pan; grill 6 to 8 minutes or until lightly browned, turning after 4 minutes.

5. Meanwhile, pour remaining ½ cup stir-fry sauce into large nonstick skillet; heat over medium-high heat. Add carrots and snow peas; cook and stir 4 to 6 minutes or until crisp-tender. Add rice; stir to combine.

6. Divide rice mixture between 4 plates; top each with tofu triangle.

Makes 4 servings

chicken saltimbocca

gluten-free | dairy-free | egg-free | nut-free

¼ cup fresh basil leaves, coarsely chopped

2 tablespoons chopped fresh chives

2 teaspoons extra virgin olive oil

1 clove garlic, minced

½ teaspoon dried oregano

½ teaspoon dried sage

4 boneless skinless chicken breasts (about 4 ounces each)

2 slices smoked ham, cut in half

½ cup chicken broth

1 cup pasta sauce

2 cups cooked spaghetti squash, warmed (see Tip)

1. Combine basil, chives, oil, garlic, oregano and sage in small bowl. Lightly pound chicken breasts between 2 pieces of plastic wrap with flat side of meat mallet to ½- to ¾-inch thickness. Spread one quarter of herb mixture over each chicken breast. Place ham slice over herb mixture; roll up to enclose filling. Secure with toothpicks.

2. Spray medium nonstick skillet with cooking spray. Heat skillet over medium-high heat. Cook chicken breasts, seam side up, 2 to 3 minutes or until browned. Turn chicken; cook 2 to 3 minutes or until browned on all sides. Add broth; reduce heat to medium-low. Cover and simmer 20 to 25 minutes or until chicken is cooked through.

3. Remove chicken to cutting board, leaving liquid in skillet. Let chicken cool 5 minutes. Add pasta sauce to skillet; cook over medium-low heat 2 to 3 minutes or until heated through, stirring occasionally.

4. Remove toothpicks from chicken and cut crosswise into slices. Serve chicken on spaghetti squash topped with pasta sauce.

Makes 4 servings

tip: To quickly cook spaghetti squash, cut a 2½-pound squash in half lengthwise with a sharp knife. Remove the seeds from each half. Place halves cut sides down in a microwavable baking dish. Add ½ cup water, cover with plastic wrap and cook on HIGH 10 to 15 minutes or until the squash is soft. Let cool 10 to 15 minutes. Scrape out squash "strands" with a fork. A 2½-pound squash yields about 4 cups cooked squash.

gluten-free pizza

gluten-free | egg-free | nut-free

1 ¾ cups gluten-free all-purpose flour blend

1 ½ cups white rice flour

2 teaspoons sugar

1 envelope (¼ ounce) rapid-rise yeast

1 ½ teaspoons salt

1 ½ teaspoons Italian seasoning

1 teaspoon baking powder

½ teaspoon xanthan gum

1 ¼ cups hot water (120°F)

2 tablespoons olive oil

Toppings: pizza sauce, fresh mozzarella, sliced tomatoes, fresh basil, grated Parmesan cheese

1. Combine dry ingredients in bowl of stand mixer. With mixer running on low speed, add water in steady stream until soft dough ball forms. Add olive oil and beat 2 minutes. Transfer to rice-floured surface and knead 2 minutes or until dough holds together in a smooth ball.

2. Place dough in oiled bowl; turn to coat. Cover; let rise 30 minutes in warm place. (Dough will increase in size but not double.)

3. Preheat oven to 400°F. Line pizza pan or baking sheet with foil. Punch down dough and transfer to center of prepared pan. Spread dough as thin as possible (about ⅛ inch thick) using dampened hands. Bake 5 to 7 minutes or until crust begins to color. (Crust may crack in spots.)

4. Top pizza with favorite toppings. Bake 10 to 15 minutes or until cheese is melted and pizza is cooked through. **Makes 4 to 6 servings**

gluten-free | dairy-free | egg-free

Top pizza with dairy-free cheese alternative or omit cheese and top with vegan pesto (see page 65) and vegetables.

italian vegetarian grill

 gluten-free | egg-free | nut-free

1 large bell pepper, cut into strips

1 medium zucchini, cut lengthwise into ½-inch thick pieces

½ pound asparagus (about 10 spears)

1 red onion, cut into ½-inch-thick rounds

¼ cup olive oil

1 teaspoon salt, divided

½ teaspoon Italian seasoning

½ teaspoon black pepper, divided

4 cups water

1 cup uncooked polenta

4 ounces goat cheese

1. Arrange bell peppers, zucchini and asparagus in single layer on baking sheet. To hold onion together securely, pierce slices horizontally with metal skewers. Place on baking sheet. Combine oil, ½ teaspoon salt, Italian seasoning and ¼ teaspoon black pepper in small bowl. Brush mixture generously over vegetables, turning to coat all sides.

2. Prepare grill for direct cooking. Meanwhile, bring water to a boil with remaining ½ teaspoon salt in large saucepan. Whisk in polenta gradually. Reduce heat to medium. Cook, stirring constantly, until polenta thickens and begins to pull away from side of pan. Stir in remaining ¼ teaspoon black pepper. Keep warm.

3. Place vegetables on grid; grill over medium-high heat, covered, 10 to 15 minutes or until tender, turning once. Place bell pepper in large bowl. Cover; let stand 5 minutes to loosen skin. When cool enough to handle, peel off charred skin. Cut all vegetables into bite-size pieces.

4. Serve polenta topped with vegetables; sprinkle with goat cheese.

Makes 4 servings

gluten-free | dairy-free | egg-free | nut-free

Omit the goat cheese or replace it with your favorite dairy-free cheese alternative.

midweek moussaka

gluten-free | egg-free | nut-free

1 eggplant (about 1 pound), cut into ¼-inch slices

2 tablespoons olive oil

1 pound ground beef

1 can (about 14 ounces) stewed tomatoes, drained

¼ cup red wine

2 tablespoons tomato paste

2 teaspoons sugar

¾ teaspoon salt

½ teaspoon dried oregano

¼ teaspoon ground cinnamon

¼ teaspoon black pepper

⅛ teaspoon ground allspice

4 ounces cream cheese

¼ cup milk

¼ cup grated Parmesan cheese

Additional ground cinnamon (optional)

1. Preheat broiler. Spray 8-inch square baking dish with nonstick cooking spray.

2. Line baking sheet with foil. Arrange eggplant slices on foil, overlapping slightly if necessary. Brush with oil; broil 5 to 6 inches from heat 4 minutes on each side. Reduce oven temperature to 350°F.

3. Meanwhile, brown beef in large skillet over medium-high heat, stirring to break up meat. Drain fat. Add tomatoes, wine, tomato paste, sugar, salt, oregano, cinnamon, pepper and allspice. Bring to a boil, breaking up large pieces of tomato with spoon. Reduce heat to medium-low; cover and simmer 10 minutes,

4. Place cream cheese and milk in small microwavable bowl. Cover and microwave on HIGH 1 minute or until melted. Stir with fork until smooth.

5. Arrange half of eggplant slices in prepared baking dish. Spoon half of meat sauce over eggplant; sprinkle with half of Parmesan cheese. Repeat layers. Spoon cream cheese mixture evenly on top. Bake 20 minutes or until top begins to crack slightly. Sprinkle lightly with cinnamon, if desired. Let stand 10 minutes before serving. **Makes 4 servings**

spring vegetable ragoût

gluten-free | dairy-free | egg-free | nut-free

1 tablespoon olive oil

2 leeks, thinly sliced

3 cloves garlic, minced

1 cup vegetable broth

1 package (10 ounces) frozen corn

½ pound yellow squash, halved lengthwise and cut into ½-inch pieces (about 1¼ cups)

1 cup frozen shelled edamame (soybeans)

1 bag (4 ounces) shredded carrots

3 cups small cherry tomatoes, halved

1 teaspoon dried tarragon

1 teaspoon dried basil

1 teaspoon dried oregano

Salt and black pepper

Minced fresh parsley (optional)

1. Heat oil in large skillet over medium heat. Add leeks and garlic; cook and stir just until fragrant. Add broth, corn, squash, edamame and carrots; cook, stirring occasionally, until squash is tender.

2. Add tomatoes, tarragon, basil and oregano; stir well. Reduce heat and simmer, covered, 2 minutes or until tomatoes are soft.

3. Season with salt and pepper. Garnish with parsley.

Makes 6 servings

TIP Living with allergies is an opportunity to add new and different vegetables to your diet. It's easy to add flavor, variety and color. Try Asian eggplant, edamame, parsnips, chard or kale. Chances are you'll find healthy new flavors you like with a bit of experimentation.

safe kid stuff

chili con corny

gluten-free | egg-free | nut-free

1 tablespoon vegetable oil

½ cup finely chopped onion

1 pound ground turkey

1 can (about 15 ounces) kidney beans, rinsed and drained

1 can (about 14 ounces) diced tomatoes

1 can (11 ounces) corn, drained

1 can (8 ounces) tomato sauce

2 teaspoons gluten-free chili seasoning mix or taco seasoning

1 teaspoon salt

1 teaspoon ground cumin

¾ cup (3 ounces) shredded Cheddar cheese

2 cups corn chips

1. Heat oil in large skillet over medium heat. Add onion; cook and stir 2 minutes. Add turkey; cook, stirring to break up meat, until cooked through.

2. Stir in beans, tomatoes, corn, tomato sauce, chili seasoning, salt and cumin. Bring to a simmer; cook and stir 10 minutes.

3. Serve chili topped with cheese and corn chips.   Makes 4 servings

 gluten-free | dairy-free | egg-free | nut-free

Omit the Cheddar cheese or substitute your favorite dairy-free cheese alternative.

magic rainbow pops

gluten-free | egg-free | nut-free

1 envelope (¼ ounce) unflavored gelatin

¼ cup cold water

½ cup boiling water

1 container (6 ounces) raspberry or strawberry yogurt

1 small can (about 8 ounces) apricots or peaches with juice

1 container (6 ounces) lemon or orange yogurt

Pop molds

1. Combine gelatin and cold water in 2-cup glass measuring cup. Let stand 5 minutes to soften. Add boiling water. Stir until gelatin is completely dissolved. Cool.

2. For first layer, combine raspberry yogurt and ¼ cup gelatin mixture in small bowl; stir until completely blended. Fill each pop mold about one third full with raspberry mixture. Freeze 30 to 60 minutes until slightly frozen.

3. Meanwhile, place apricots with juice and ¼ cup gelatin mixture in blender. Cover; process 20 seconds or until smooth. Set aside.

4. For second layer, combine lemon yogurt and remaining ¼ cup gelatin mixture in small bowl. Stir until completely blended. Pour lemon mixture over raspberry layer in each mold. Freeze 30 to 60 minutes or until slightly frozen.*

5. For third layer, pour apricot mixture into each mold. Cover each pop with mold top; freeze 2 to 5 hours or until pops are firm.

6. To remove pops from molds, run warm water over bottom of pop. Press firmly on bottom to release. (Do not twist or pull the pop stick.)

Makes about 6 pops

Pour any extra mixture into small paper cups. Freeze as directed in the Tip.

tip: Three-ounce paper or plastic cups can be used in place of the molds. Make the layers as directed or put a single flavor in each cup. Freeze the mixture about 1 hour, then insert a wooden stick into the center of each cup. Freeze completely. Peel cup off each pop to serve.

gluten-free | dairy-free | egg-free | nut-free

Replace regular yogurt with dairy-free soy or rice yogurt.

allergy-free birthday cake

gluten-free | dairy-free | egg-free | nut-free

3 cups gluten-free all-purpose flour blend, plus extra for cake pans

2 cups sugar

6 tablespoons unsweetened cocoa powder

2 teaspoons baking soda

2 teaspoons xanthan gum

1 teaspoon salt

2 cups chocolate soymilk

½ cup plus 2 tablespoons vegetable oil

2 tablespoons cider vinegar

1 teaspoon vanilla

No-Butter Buttercream Frosting (page 84)

1. Preheat oven to 350°F. Grease 2 (9-inch) round cake pans with shortening or dairy-free margarine. Sprinkle with gluten-free baking mix; tap out excess.

2. Whisk together gluten-free flour, sugar, cocoa powder, baking soda, xanthan gum and salt in large bowl. Combine soymilk, oil, vinegar and vanilla in small bowl.

3. Pour wet ingredients into dry ingredients; stir until smooth, being sure to incorporate ingredients at bottom of bowl. Immediately pour into prepared pans.

4. Bake 25 to 30 minutes or until toothpick inserted into centers comes out clean. (Middle of cake may look darker than edges.) Cool in pans 5 minutes. Carefully invert onto wire rack to cool completely. Meanwhile prepare frosting.

5. Fill and frost cake; decorate as desired.   Makes 10 servings

dairy-free | egg-free | nut-free

Replace the gluten-free all-purpose flour blend with regular all-purpose flour. Omit the xanthan gum. Proceed as directed.

continued on page 84

allergy-free birthday cake, continued

no-butter buttercream frosting

gluten-free | dairy-free | egg-free | nut-free

½ cup (1 stick) dairy-free margarine (do not use spread)
2 teaspoons vanilla
½ cup unsweetened cocoa powder
3 to 4 cups powdered sugar
4 to 6 tablespoons soy creamer

1. Beat margarine with electric mixer at medium speed until light and fluffy. Add vanilla.

2. Gradually beat in cocoa and powdered sugar. Beat in soy creamer, 1 tablespoon at a time, until spreading consistency is reached.

tip: For white frosting, omit cocoa; tint as desired.

tofu orange dream

gluten-free | dairy-free | egg-free | nut-free

½ cup soft tofu
½ cup orange juice
1 container (about 2½ ounces) baby food carrots
2 tablespoons honey or 1 tablespoon sugar
¼ teaspoon grated fresh ginger
2 to 3 ice cubes

Place all ingredients in blender. Blend 15 seconds or until smooth. Pour into glass; serve immediately.   Makes 1 serving

scrambled egg & zucchini pie

gluten-free | nut-free

2 teaspoons butter
1 small zucchini, chopped (about ¼ cup)
2 eggs
2 tablespoons grated Parmesan or Cheddar cheese
¼ teaspoon salt

1. Preheat oven to 350°F. Melt butter in small ovenproof skillet over medium-high heat. Add zucchini; cook and stir 2 to 3 minutes or until crisp-tender.

2. Meanwhile, beat eggs in small bowl. Stir in cheese and salt.

3. Reduce heat to low and add egg mixture to skillet with zucchini; stir gently. Cook, undisturbed, 4 to 5 minutes or until eggs begin to set around edges.

4. Transfer skillet to oven and bake 5 minutes or until eggs are set. Cut into wedges to serve. *Makes 4 servings*

gluten-free | dairy-free | nut-free

Substitute dairy-free margarine for the butter and a dairy-free cheese alternative for the Parmesan cheese.

kitty cat pancakes

gluten-free I dairy-free I nut-free

1 ¼ cups rice flour

¼ cup tapioca flour

¼ cup cornstarch

1 tablespoon sugar

1 ½ teaspoons baking powder

½ teaspoon baking soda

½ teaspoon salt

½ teaspoon xanthan gum

1 cup plain soymilk

2 eggs

3 tablespoons vegetable oil

Juice of ½ lemon

½ teaspoon vanilla

Decorations: dried cherries or raisins, thin slivers of red-skinned apple

1. Combine rice flour, tapioca flour, cornstarch, sugar, baking powder, baking soda, salt and xanthan gum in large bowl.

2. Stir in soymilk, eggs, oil, lemon juice and vanilla until thick batter forms. For thinner pancakes, add additional soymilk.

3. Lightly grease griddle or nonstick skillet; heat over medium heat. Pour about ½ cup batter onto griddle. Spread batter to oval shape with back of spoon. Spread 2 points of batter upwards to make kitty ears, adding small amount of additional batter if needed.

4. Create eyes, nose and mouth by placing dried cherries or raisins gently on batter. For whiskers, place slivers of apple, peel side showing, onto batter. When surface of pancake becomes dull and bubbles appear (2 to 3 minutes), turn pancake. Cook 30 seconds to 1 minute or until lightly browned.

5. Repeat with remaining batter. Serve warm with maple syrup, if desired.

Makes about 8 pancakes

dairy-free | nut-free

Substitute 2 cups biscuit baking mix for rice flour, tapioca flour and cornstarch. Omit xanthan gum.

yam yums

gluten-free I egg-free I nut-free

2 large sweet potatoes
¼ cup maple syrup (not pancake syrup)
2 tablespoons orange juice
2 tablespoons butter, melted
⅛ teaspoon ground nutmeg
 Salt and black pepper

1. Preheat oven to 350°F. Line baking sheet with foil.

2. Cut scrubbed, unpeeled sweet potatoes crosswise into ½-inch-thick slices. Place slices on cutting board; use small metal cookie cutters (1½ inches in diameter) to cut shapes and letters from slices. Or cut out shapes with sharp knife.

3. Combine maple syrup, orange juice and butter in small bowl. Arrange potato shapes in single layer on prepared baking sheet. Season both sides with nutmeg, salt and pepper. Brush both sides generously with maple syrup mixture.

4. Bake 20 to 30 minutes or until tender, turning pieces once and basting with remaining syrup mixture. **Makes about 4 servings**

gluten-free I dairy-free I egg-free I nut-free

Replace butter with dairy-free margarine.

TIP Finding out that they have a food allergy is tough on young children. They need to understand the foods to be avoided and how to eat safely when parents are not around. At home they can enjoy foods that are fun and healthy. This recipe for Yam Yums will be a hit with non-allergic friends, too.

flourless fried chicken tenders

 gluten-free | nut-free

1 ½ cups chickpea flour*
1 ½ teaspoons Italian seasoning
 1 teaspoon salt
 ½ teaspoon black pepper
 ⅛ teaspoon ground red pepper
 ¾ cup plus 2 to 4 tablespoons water
  Oil for frying
 1 pound chicken tenders, cut in half if large
  Curry Mayo Dipping Sauce (optional)

Chickpea flour is also called garbanzo flour. It is found in the specialty food section of most supermarkets.

1. Sift chickpea flour into medium bowl. Stir in Italian seasoning, salt, black pepper and red pepper. Gradually whisk in ¾ cup water to make smooth batter. Whisk in additional water by tablespoons if needed until batter is consistency of heavy cream.

2. Meanwhile, add oil to large heavy skillet or Dutch oven to ¾-inch depth. Heat over medium-high heat until drop of batter placed in oil sizzles (350°F).

3. Pat chicken pieces dry. Dip pieces into batter with tongs; let excess fall back into bowl. Ease chicken gently into oil; fry 2 to 3 minutes per side until slightly browned and chicken is cooked through. Fry in batches; do not crowd pan. Drain on paper towels. Serve warm with Curry Mayo Dipping Sauce, if desired.

Makes 4 servings

curry mayo dipping sauce: Combine ½ cup mayonnaise, ¼ cup sour cream and ½ teaspoon curry powder in small bowl. Stir in 2 tablespoons minced fresh cilantro.

 gluten-free | dairy-free | egg-free | nut-free

Prepare the dipping sauce with vegan mayonnaise (dairy-free, egg-free) and dairy-free sour cream or serve the chicken tenders with salsa or barbecue sauce.

giggle jiggles

gluten-free | dairy-free | egg-free | nut-free

2 cups pomegranate juice, divided
2 envelopes (¼ ounce each) unflavored gelatin
½ cup blueberries

1. Combine ½ cup juice and gelatin in small glass measuring cup. Stir to mix well. Let stand 5 minutes to soften.

2. Bring remaining 1½ cups juice to a boil in small saucepan. Remove from heat; stir in softened gelatin mixture until dissolved.

3. Spray 8- or 9-inch square baking dish or pan lightly with nonstick cooking spray. Pour warm gelatin mixture into dish. Let cool to room temperature. Add blueberries. Refrigerate 3 hours or until firm.

4. Dip bottom of dish in warm water 15 seconds. Cut gelatin into small shapes with cookie cutters. Lift shapes from pan. Reserve scraps for snacking or add them to a fruit cup.

5. Store leftovers tightly covered in refrigerator.

Makes 2 to 4 servings

TIP You can help keep your allergic child safe by taking special precautions. Offer to provide safe snacks to keep on hand at the homes of close friends so visiting will be easier and your child will feel included. Be especially careful when a celebration is involved. It's not easy for any child (or adult for that matter!) to refuse a piece of pizza or a slice of birthday cake. Make sure parents who will be feeding your allergic child understand the seriousness of the problem. Provide alternatives for your child to enjoy if that will help. Food allergies and intolerances are on the increase and understanding of them has improved. Don't hesitate to speak up and teach your child to be confident about asking the right questions when he or she is offered any food.

kids' oasis

dairy-free | egg-free | nut-free

hummus

- 2 cans (about 15 ounces each) chickpeas, rinsed and drained
- ¼ cup tahini (sesame paste)
- Juice from 1 lemon
- 1 tablespoon olive oil
- 3 cloves garlic, minced
- ½ teaspoon salt
- ¼ teaspoon ground black pepper

broccoli trees and couscous sand

- 2 cups broccoli florets
- 1 box (10 ounces) couscous, plus ingredients to prepare couscous
- Green onions and chives (optional)

1. To make hummus, place chickpeas, tahini, lemon juice, oil, garlic, salt and pepper in food processor. Process 2 to 3 minutes or until coarse paste is formed, stopping processor and scraping side of bowl occasionally. Refrigerate until ready to serve.

2. Cook broccoli florets in boiling salted water until crisp-tender; drain. Meanwhile, prepare couscous according to package directions.

3. To make each oasis, spread ¼ cup hummus in center of plate. Insert broccoli "trees" and surround with couscous "sand." Drizzle with additional olive oil and garnish with green onions and chives, if desired. Serve with pita bread.   **Makes about 12 servings**

allergy-free mac & cheez

gluten-free | dairy-free | egg-free | nut-free

cheez powder

2 tablespoons flaked nutritional yeast*

4 teaspoons sweet rice flour**

¾ teaspoon salt

½ teaspoon onion powder

½ teaspoon garlic powder

¼ teaspoon mustard powder

pasta

8 ounces gluten-free penne, rotini or other small pasta shape

½ cup soymilk

Extras: cooked ground beef or chicken, cooked peas, broccoli or carrots

Nutritional yeast can be found in health food stores and some supermarkets. It is NOT similar to regular yeast or brewer's yeast.

**Sweet rice flour is sometimes labeled glutinous rice flour (although it is gluten-free) or mochiko (the Japanese term). It is available in the Asian section of large supermarkets, at Asian grocers and on-line.*

1. Bring large saucepan of water to a boil. Meanwhile, prepare Cheez Powder. Mix nutritional yeast, rice flour, salt, onion powder, garlic powder and mustard powder in small bowl until completely combined.*

2. Cook pasta in boiling water according to package directions until al dente. Reserve ½ cup pasta cooking water; drain pasta. Oil pasta lightly if needed to prevent sticking.

3. Stir Cheez Powder and soymilk in large saucepan until smooth. Add pasta; cook and stir over medium heat 1 to 2 minutes. Add 4 to 6 tablespoons pasta cooking water and continue cooking 2 minutes or until sauce coats pasta. Add extras, if desired, and heat through.

Makes 4 servings

Cheez Powder may be prepared in advance and stored in a covered container at room temperature. You may double or triple the quantities and save extra Cheez Powder for future use.

tickle sticks

 gluten-free | egg-free | nut-free

    1 pound watermelon
    1 container (6 ounces) low-fat plain yogurt
    2 teaspoons honey
    Grated peel and juice of 1 lime

1. Cut watermelon into 3×½-inch sticks. Remove and discard seeds.

2. Combine yogurt, honey, lime peel and lime juice in small bowl. Serve with Tickle Sticks for dipping.   **Makes 4 to 6 servings**

 gluten-free | dairy-free | egg-free | nut-free

Substitute plain or vanilla soy yogurt for regular yogurt.

mini s'mores pies

gluten-free... dairy-free | egg-free | nut-free

    6 miniature graham cracker pie crusts
    ½ cup dairy-free semisweet chocolate chips, divided
    ¾ cup miniature marshmallows

1. Preheat oven to 325°F. Place pie crusts on baking sheet.

2. Divide ¼ cup chocolate chips among pie crusts. Sprinkle marshmallows over chocolate chips. Top with remaining ¼ cup chocolate chips.

3. Bake 3 to 5 minutes or until marshmallows start to turn golden brown.
                                          Makes 6 servings

corny face

gluten-free | egg-free | nut-free

Nonstick cooking spray

1 corn tortilla

1 slice provolone cheese or 3 tablespoons shredded Cheddar cheese

½ large dill pickle (cut lengthwise at an angle)

2 slices cucumber

2 pitted black olives

2 tablespoons shredded carrot

1. Lightly spray skillet with cooking spray; heat over medium heat. Place tortilla in skillet; top with cheese. Heat 1 minute; fold tortilla in half, enclosing cheese.

2. Cook tortilla 1 minute per side or until cheese is melted and tortilla is lightly browned. Place tortilla on plate, rounded side facing outer edge of plate. Place pickle at center of plate, partially overlapping tortilla, for nose. Place cucumber slices above tortilla one on each side of pickle. Top cucumber with olives to resemble eyes. Mound shredded carrot over cucumber slices to resemble eyebrows.   **Makes 1 serving**

TIP

Unfortunately most common allergens are also very common ingredients in recipes. Finding good substitutions is sometimes easy (soymilk for regular milk) and sometimes impossible. Whether or not you can make a substitution depends on what function the ingredient provides. For instance, gluten-free bread requires a whole new recipe, not just a one-to-one replacement of the flour, because gluten is what provides bread's structure. An egg replacement, such as soy yogurt, may work well when you are baking muffins, but it won't work if you want scrambled eggs. In some cases, it's easier to find a new recipe than to recreate a familiar one.

from the oven

basic oatmeal cookies

dairy-free | egg-free | nut-free

   2 cups old-fashioned oats
1 1/3 cups all-purpose flour
   1 teaspoon ground cinnamon
   3/4 teaspoon baking soda
   1/2 teaspoon baking powder
   1/2 teaspoon salt
   1/2 teaspoon cornstarch* (optional)
   1 cup packed light brown sugar
   3/4 cup (1 1/2 sticks) dairy-free margarine, softened
   1/2 cup granulated sugar
   1/4 cup silken tofu, lightly beaten

Adding cornstarch will make the cookies a bit less puffy when baked.

1. Preheat oven to 350°F. Combine oats, flour, cinnamon, baking soda, baking powder, salt and cornstarch, if desired, in medium bowl.

2. Beat brown sugar, margarine and granulated sugar in large bowl with electric mixer at medium speed until light and fluffy. Add tofu; beat until blended. Gradually add oat mixture; beat just until blended

3. Drop dough by tablespoonfuls about 2 inches apart onto cookie sheet. Bake 11 to 15 minutes or until puffed and golden. Cool 5 minutes on cookie sheets; transfer to wire racks.   **Makes 3 dozen cookies**

loaded banana bread

dairy-free | egg-free

6 tablespoons vegetable shortening

⅓ cup packed light brown sugar

⅓ cup granulated sugar

¼ cup silken tofu, lightly beaten

3 ripe bananas, mashed

½ teaspoon vanilla

1½ cups all-purpose flour

2½ teaspoons baking powder

½ teaspoon salt

1 can (8 ounces) crushed pineapple, drained (optional)

⅓ cup flaked coconut

⅓ cup dairy-free semisweet chocolate chips

⅓ cup chopped walnuts

1. Preheat oven to 350°F. Coat 9×5-inch loaf pan with nonstick cooking spray.

2. Beat shortening, brown sugar and granulated sugar in large bowl with electric mixer at medium speed until light and fluffy. Beat in tofu; scrape down bowl. Add bananas and vanilla; beat just until just combined.

3. Stir together flour, baking powder and salt in small bowl. Gradually beat flour mixture into banana mixture just until combined. Stir in pineapple, if desired, coconut and chocolate chips.

4. Spoon batter into prepared pan. Top with walnuts. Bake 50 to 60 minutes or until toothpick inserted into center comes out almost clean. Cool 5 minutes in pan; transfer to wire rack.   Makes 1 loaf

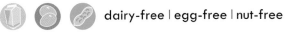 **dairy-free | egg-free | nut-free**

Omit the chopped walnuts in step 4.

gluten-free | dairy-free

Substitute 1½ cups gluten-free all-purpose flour blend for 1½ cups all-purpose flour. Substitute 2 eggs for the tofu in step 2. Add 1 teaspoon xanthan gum to the dry ingredients in step 3. Bake about 1 hour or until toothpick inserted into center comes out almost clean. If banana bread browns too quickly, cover with foil for the last 10 to 15 minutes.

whole wheat brownies

dairy-free | egg-free | nut-free

½ cup whole wheat flour
½ teaspoon baking soda
¼ teaspoon salt
½ cup (1 stick) dairy-free margarine
1 cup packed brown sugar
½ cup unsweetened cocoa powder
½ cup dairy-free semisweet chocolate chips
1 teaspoon vanilla
½ cup silken tofu, lightly beaten

1. Preheat oven to 350°F. Spray 8-inch square baking pan with nonstick cooking spray. Combine flour, baking soda and salt in small bowl.

2. Melt margarine in large saucepan over low heat. Add brown sugar; cook and stir about 4 minutes or until sugar is completely dissolved and smooth. Remove pan from heat; sift in cocoa and stir until combined. Add flour mixture and stir until smooth. (Mixture will be thick.)

3. Stir in chocolate chips and vanilla. Beat in tofu until mixture is smooth. Spoon batter into prepared pan.

4. Bake 25 minutes or until toothpick inserted into center comes out almost clean.

Makes 8 brownies

 gluten-free | dairy-free | nut-free

Substitute ¼ cup cornstarch and ¼ cup brown rice flour for whole wheat flour. Increase baking soda to 1 teaspoon. Substitute 2 eggs for ½ cup tofu. Bake 25 to 30 minutes or until toothpick inserted into center comes out almost clean.

brazilian cheese rolls
(pão de queijo)

 gluten-free | nut-free

1 cup whole milk
¼ cup (½ stick) butter, cut into pieces
¼ cup vegetable oil
2 cups plus 2 tablespoons tapioca flour
2 eggs
1 cup grated Parmesan cheese or other dry, firm cheese

1. Preheat oven to 350°F.

2. Combine milk, butter and oil in large saucepan. Bring to a boil over medium heat, stirring to melt butter. Remove from heat; stir in tapioca flour. (Mixture will be thick and stretchy.)

3. Beat in eggs, 1 at a time, and cheese. (Mixture will be very stiff.) Cool mixture in pan until easy to handle.

4. Roll golf-ball-size portions of dough into balls with tapioca-floured hands. Place on baking sheet about 1 inch apart.

5. Bake 20 to 25 minutes or until puffed and golden. Serve warm.

Makes about 20 rolls

TIP These moist, chewy, Brazilian rolls are made with tapioca flour instead of wheat flour, so are perfect for gluten-free diets. In Brazil they are popular at breakfast, lunch or dinner. Tapioca flour can be found in most large supermarkets and is also readily available in Asian markets where it is often labeled tapioca starch. It comes from the cassava root (also called yuca or manioc), which is also the source of the tapioca used in puddings.

easy orange cake

  dairy-free | egg-free | nut-free

1½ cups all-purpose flour
1 cup sugar
1 teaspoon baking soda
½ teaspoon salt
Grated peel of 1 orange
1 cup orange juice
5 tablespoons vegetable oil
Orange No-Butter Buttercream Frosting (recipe follows)
Candied orange peel (optional)

1. Preheat oven to 350°F. Spray 8-inch square or 9-inch round cake pan with nonstick cooking spray.

2. Combine flour, sugar, baking soda, salt and orange peel in medium bowl. Combine orange juice and oil in small bowl or measuring cup. Add to flour mixture and stir until smooth. Spread in prepared pan.

3. Bake 30 minutes or until toothpick inserted into center comes out clean. Meanwhile, prepare Orange No-Butter Buttercream Frosting.

4. Cool cake in pan on wire rack; frost and garnish with candied orange peel, if desired. **Makes about 6 servings**

gluten-free | dairy-free | egg-free | nut-free

Substitute 1½ cups gluten-free all-purpose flour blend for all-purpose flour and add 1 teaspoon xanthan gum to the dry ingredients. Proceed as directed.

orange no-butter buttercream frosting

gluten-free | dairy-free | egg-free | nut-free

½ cup (1 stick) dairy-free margarine (do not use spread)

2 teaspoons grated orange peel

2 tablespoons orange juice

1 teaspoon vanilla

4 cups powdered sugar

4 to 6 tablespoons soy creamer

1. Beat margarine with electric mixer at medium speed until light and fluffy. Add orange peel, orange juice and vanilla.

2. Gradually beat in powdered sugar. Beat in soy creamer, 1 tablespoonful at a time, until spreading consistency is reached.   **Makes about 2 cups**

TIP Margarine that is totally dairy-free can be hard to find. Many—in fact, most— margarines contain some sort of milk product, such as casein or whey. The labels of these products must show that they contain milk per FDA rules. To find a truly dairy-free margarine, check health food stores and look for a spread that is labeled "vegan." For frosting you'll need a stick-type of margarine, not a spread or an oil.

whole wheat pumpkin muffins

 dairy-free | egg-free

1 ½ cups whole wheat flour
¼ cup sugar
1 teaspoon salt
1 teaspoon ground allspice
1 teaspoon ground nutmeg
¾ teaspoon baking powder
½ teaspoon baking soda
¾ cup canned pumpkin
½ cup canola oil
½ cup honey
½ cup frozen apple juice concentrate
½ cup chopped walnuts
½ cup golden raisins

1. Preheat oven to 350°F. Grease 10 standard (2¾-inch) muffin cups or line with paper baking cups.

2. Combine flour, sugar, salt, allspice, nutmeg, baking powder and baking soda in large bowl; mix well. Add pumpkin, oil, honey and apple juice concentrate; mix well. Stir in walnuts and raisins.

3. Spoon batter into prepared muffin cups. Bake 12 to 15 minutes or until toothpick inserted into centers comes out clean. Transfer to wire rack to cool completely. **Makes 12 muffins**

 dairy-free | egg-free | nut-free

Omit the walnuts, or replace them with sunflower seeds or flaked coconut, if tolerated.

boston black coffee bread

dairy-free | egg-free | nut-free

½ cup rye flour

½ cup cornmeal

½ cup whole wheat flour

1 teaspoon baking soda

½ teaspoon salt

¾ cup strong brewed coffee, room temperature or cold

⅓ cup molasses

¼ cup canola oil

¾ cup raisins

1. Preheat oven to 325°F. Grease and flour 9×4-inch loaf pan.

2. Combine rye flour, cornmeal, whole wheat flour, baking soda and salt in mixing bowl. Stir in coffee, molasses and oil until mixture forms thick batter. Fold in raisins.

3. Pour batter into prepared pan. Bake 50 minutes or until toothpick inserted into center comes out clean. Cool completely in pan on wire rack. Serve with dairy-free cream cheese substitute, if desired.

Makes 1 loaf

TIP Replacing butter with oil in baking recipes works best when the recipe is for a quick bread or muffin with a moist, dense texture or for a cookie. In cake recipes, creaming the butter with sugar provides lift and lightness that can't be achieved with vegetable oils. Biscuits and pastries rely on butter for their flaky texture, as well as flavor. To replace the butter in recipes for cake, biscuits or pastry, use a dairy-free stick margarine or shortening that is semi-solid at room temperature for best results.

oat-apricot snack cake

dairy-free I egg-free I nut-free

1 ½ cups all-purpose flour
1 teaspoon baking soda
1 teaspoon ground cinnamon
½ teaspoon salt
1 container (6 ounces) plain soy yogurt
¾ cup packed brown sugar
½ cup granulated sugar
⅓ cup vegetable oil
¼ cup silken tofu, lightly beaten
4 to 5 tablespoons orange juice, divided
2 teaspoons vanilla
2 cups old-fashioned oats
1 cup chopped dried apricots
1 cup powdered sugar

1. Preheat oven to 350°F. Spray 13×9-inch baking pan with nonstick cooking spray. Combine flour, baking soda, cinnamon and salt in medium bowl.

2. Whisk together yogurt, brown sugar, granulated sugar, oil, tofu, 2 tablespoons orange juice and vanilla in large bowl. Stir in flour mixture, oats and apricots until combined.

3. Spread batter in prepared pan. Bake 20 to 25 minutes or until toothpick inserted into center comes out clean. Cool completely in pan on wire rack.

4. Whisk remaining 2 tablespoons orange juice into powdered sugar. Add additional 1 tablespoon orange juice, if needed. Drizzle glaze over cake.   Makes 24 servings

double chocolate cupcakes

dairy-free | egg-free | nut-free

1 cup all-purpose flour
½ cup unsweetened cocoa powder
1 teaspoon baking soda
½ teaspoon salt
1 cup soymilk
1½ teaspoons cider vinegar
¾ cup granulated sugar
⅓ cup vegetable oil
1 teaspoon vanilla
¼ cup dairy-free semisweet chocolate chips
    Powdered sugar

1. Preheat oven to 350°F. Grease 10 standard (2¾-inch) muffin cups or line with paper baking cups.

2. Sift together flour, cocoa powder, baking soda and salt in small bowl. Pour soymilk into large bowl and stir in vinegar. Let mixture sit 2 minutes.

3. Add sugar, oil and vanilla to soymilk mixture; whisk until foamy. Add flour mixture gradually, whisking until smooth. Stir in chocolate chips.

4. Pour batter into prepared muffin cups. Bake 15 to 18 minutes or until toothpick inserted into centers comes out clean. Sprinkle with powdered sugar before serving.   **Makes 10 cupcakes**

sweets & treats

coconut panna cotta

gluten-free | dairy-free | egg-free

3 tablespoons water
1 envelope (¼ ounce) unflavored gelatin
1 can (14½ ounces) unsweetened coconut milk*
½ cup sugar
½ teaspoon vanilla
4 tablespoons toasted flaked coconut*
2 slices (½ inch thick) fresh pineapple, cut into pieces

Many who suffer from tree-nut or peanut allergies are able to eat coconut products. However, please consult your allergist if you are in doubt. (See page 10 of the introduction.)

1. Place water in small bowl and sprinkle with gelatin; set aside.

2. Heat coconut milk, sugar and vanilla in medium saucepan over medium heat. Cook and stir until sugar is dissolved and mixture is smooth. *Do not boil.* Add gelatin mixture; stir until gelatin is completely dissolved.

3. Pour mixture evenly into four 5-ounce custard cups. Refrigerate about 3 hours or until set.

4. To unmold, run knife around outside edges of cups; place cups in hot water about 30 seconds. Place serving plate over cup; invert and shake until panna cotta drops onto plate. Top each serving with 1 tablespoon toasted coconut and one fourth of pineapple pieces. Refrigerate leftovers.   Makes 4 servings

flourless peanut butter cookies

 gluten-free | dairy-free

1 cup packed light brown sugar
1 cup smooth peanut butter
1 egg, lightly beaten
½ cup semisweet chocolate chips, melted

1. Preheat oven to 350°F. Beat brown sugar, peanut butter and egg in medium bowl until blended and smooth.

2. Shape dough into 24 balls; place 2 inches apart on ungreased cookie sheets. Flatten dough slightly with fork. Bake 10 to 12 minutes or until set. Transfer to wire racks to cool. Drizzle with chocolate.

Makes 2 dozen cookies

flourless almond cookies

 gluten-free | dairy-free

1 cup granulated sugar
1 cup almond butter
1 egg, lightly beaten

1. Preheat oven to 350°F. Beat sugar, almond butter and egg in medium bowl until blended and smooth.

2. Shape dough into 24 balls; place 2 inches apart on ungreased cookie sheets. Flatten dough slightly with fork. Bake 10 to 12 minutes or until set. Transfer to wire racks to cool.

Makes 2 dozen cookies

  gluten-free | dairy-free | nut-free

Substitute 1 cup sunflower seed butter for peanut butter or almond butter. Proceed as directed.

cranberry chocolate chip
cereal squares

gluten-free | dairy-free | egg-free | nut-free

6½ cups gluten-free corn or rice cereal squares
½ cup (1 stick) dairy-free margarine
1 bag (about 10 ounces) miniature marshmallows
1 package (6 ounces) dried cranberries (about 1⅓ cups)
1 cup dairy-free semisweet chocolate chips

1. Line 13×9-inch pan with foil; spray foil with nonstick cooking spray.

2. Place 2 cups cereal in large bowl. Coarsely crush with back of large spoon or hands. Stir in cranberries.

3. Melt margarine in large saucepan over low heat. Add marshmallows; stir constantly until melted and smooth. Remove from heat; stir in remaining 4½ cups whole cereal and crushed cereal mixture until well blended. Stir in chocolate chips.

4. Press mixture into prepared pan. Cover and refrigerate 30 minutes or until firm. Remove from pan using foil; cut into squares.

Makes about 30 squares

TIP   Now that gluten-free cereals are readily available, you can use them in many different ways. Try making your own gluten-free trail mix or granola. Crushed cereal can stand in for bread crumbs as a topping on a fruit desert or even as a gluten-free breading for fish or chicken.

raisin-coconut cookies

 gluten-free | dairy-free

1¾ cups gluten-free all-purpose flour blend
2 teaspoons baking powder
½ teaspoon xanthan gum
½ teaspoon salt
1 cup (2 sticks) dairy-free margarine
½ cup granulated sugar
½ cup packed brown sugar
1 egg
1 teaspoon vanilla
2 cups flaked coconut
1½ cups raisins

1. Preheat oven to 350°F. Line cookie sheet with parchment paper.

2. Combine gluten-free flour, baking powder, xanthan gum and salt in medium bowl; whisk to blend.

3. Beat margarine and sugars in large bowl with electric mixer at medium speed about 2 minutes or until well blended. Beat in egg and vanilla. Add flour mixture; beat at low speed about 30 seconds or until just combined. Stir in coconut and raisins. Drop dough by rounded tablespoonfuls 2 inches apart onto prepared cookie sheet.

4. Bake 10 to 12 minutes or until brown around edges (centers will be light). Remove to wire rack; cool completely.

Makes about 4 dozen cookies

 dairy-free | egg-free

Replace gluten-free all-purpose flour with regular all-purpose flour. Omit the xanthan gum. Replace the egg with ¼ cup of silken tofu. Proceed as directed in steps 1 through 3. Before baking, flatten the dough with the bottom of a small glass sprayed with nonstick cooking spray. Bake as directed above.

all-american chocolate chip
cookies

 dairy-free | egg-free

2 cups all-purpose flour

1 teaspoon baking soda

½ teaspoon salt

1 cup (2 sticks) dairy-free margarine

¾ cup packed light brown sugar

½ cup granulated sugar

½ cup silken tofu, lightly beaten

1 tablespoon vanilla

2 cups dairy-free semisweet chocolate chips

1 cup chopped walnuts

1. Preheat oven to 325°F. Line cookie sheets with parchment paper. Combine flour, baking soda and salt in medium bowl.

2. Beat margarine, brown sugar, granulated sugar, tofu and vanilla in large bowl with electric mixer at medium speed until light and fluffy. Add flour mixture; beat until combined. Stir in chocolate chips and walnuts.

3. Drop dough by heaping teaspoonfuls 2 inches apart onto prepared cookie sheets. Bake 8 to 10 minutes or until light brown. Cool cookies 2 minutes on cookies sheets. Remove to wire rack; cool completely.

Makes about 4 dozen cookies

 gluten-free | dairy-free | nut-free

Substitute 2 cups of gluten-free all-purpose flour blend for 2 cups of all-purpose flour. Add 1 teaspoon of xanthan gum to the dry ingredients in step 1. Use only ½ cup (1 stick) of dairy-free margarine. Substitute 2 eggs for the silken tofu in step 2. Omit the chopped walnuts.

orange granita

gluten-free | dairy-free | egg-free | nut-free

6 small Valencia or blood oranges
¼ cup sugar
¼ cup water
⅛ teaspoon ground cinnamon

1. Cut oranges in half; squeeze juice into medium bowl and reserve empty shells. Discard seeds. Combine sugar and water in small microwavable bowl; microwave on HIGH 30 seconds to 1 minute until sugar is dissolved. Stir sugar mixture and cinnamon into juice.

2. Pour juice mixture into shallow 9-inch pan. Cover and place on flat surface in freezer. After 1 to 2 hours when ice crystals form at edges, stir with fork. Stir 2 or 3 more times at 20 to 30 minute intervals until texture of granita is like icy snow.

3. Scoop granita into orange shells to serve. Garnish with orange peel.

Makes 6 servings

variation: Add a small amount of orange liqueur to the orange juice mixture before freezing. Top with a candied orange slice or mint sprig.

crispy toffee cookies

gluten-free | dairy-free | egg-free

½ cup rice flour

½ cup dry roasted peanuts

⅛ teaspoon salt

½ cup packed brown sugar

⅓ cup dairy-free margarine

¼ cup light corn syrup

1 teaspoon vanilla

¼ cup dairy-free semisweet chocolate chips, melted (optional)

1. Preheat oven to 375°F. Line 2 cookie sheets with parchment paper.

2. Combine rice flour, peanuts and salt in food processor; process until mixture resembles coarse crumbs.

3. Combine brown sugar, margarine and corn syrup in medium saucepan; bring to a full boil over medium heat, stirring frequently. Remove from heat; stir in peanut mixture and vanilla until well blended. Return pan to low heat to keep batter warm and pliable. Spoon 6 rounded half teaspoonfuls of batter 3 inches apart on 1 prepared cookie sheet.

4. Bake exactly 4 minutes. Immediately remove from oven. (Cookies will have very light color and will appear not to be completely baked.) Remove parchment paper with cookies on top to wire rack to cool completely.

5. Continue to prepare cookies in batches of 6, baking each batch for 4 minutes. When cooled, peel cookies from parchment paper; transfer to wire racks. (Parchment paper may be re-used once cookies are removed.) Drizzle melted chocolate over cookies, if desired; let stand until set.   **Makes about 4 dozen cookies**

pumpkin oatmeal cookies

dairy-free | egg-free | nut-free

   1 cup all-purpose flour

   1 teaspoon ground cinnamon

   ½ teaspoon salt

   ½ teaspoon ground nutmeg

   ¼ teaspoon baking soda

1½ cups packed light brown sugar

   ½ cup (1 stick) dairy-free margarine

   ¼ cup silken tofu, lightly beaten

   1 teaspoon vanilla

   ½ cup solid-pack pumpkin

   2 cups old-fashioned oats

   1 cup dried cranberries (optional)

1. Preheat oven to 350°F. Line cookie sheets with parchment paper.

2. Sift flour, cinnamon, salt, nutmeg and baking soda into medium bowl. Beat brown sugar and margarine in large bowl with electric mixer at medium speed about 5 minutes or until light and fluffy.

3. Add tofu; beat until well blended. Beat in vanilla. Add pumpkin; beat at low speed until blended. Beat in flour mixture just until blended. Add oats; mix well. Stir in cranberries, if desired. Drop dough by rounded tablespoonfuls 2 inches apart onto prepared cookie sheets.

4. Bake 12 minutes or until golden brown. Cool 1 minute on cookie sheets. Remove to wire racks; cool completely.

Makes about 2 dozen cookies

mixed berry crisp

 gluten-free | egg-free

6 cups mixed berries, thawed if frozen
¾ cup packed brown sugar, divided
¼ cup minute tapioca or tapioca flour
   Juice of ½ lemon
1 teaspoon ground cinnamon
6 tablespoons cold butter, cut into pieces
½ cup rice flour
½ cup sliced almonds

1. Preheat oven to 375°F. Grease sides and bottom of 8- or 9-inch baking pan.

2. Place berries in large bowl. Add ¼ cup sugar, tapioca, lemon juice and cinnamon; stir until well combined. Let stand while preparing topping.

3. Place butter, remaining ½ cup sugar and rice flour in food processor. Pulse until coarse crumbs form. Add almonds; pulse until combined. (Leave some large pieces of almonds.)

4. Transfer berry mixture to prepared pan. Sprinkle topping over berries. Bake 20 to 30 minutes or until topping is browned and filling is bubbly.

Makes about 9 servings

 gluten-free | dairy-free | egg-free

Substitute 6 tablespoons of cold dairy-free stick margarine for the butter.

egg-free | nut-free

For the crumble topping, omit the rice flour and almonds. Place ½ cup of flour, ½ cup of old-fashioned oats and the remaining ½ cup of sugar in a food processor. Pulse to combine. Add the butter; pulse until coarse crumbs form. Sprinkle the topping over the berries and bake as directed.

cocoa raisin-chip cookies

 gluten-free | dairy-free

1½ cups gluten-free all-purpose flour blend
¼ cup unsweetened cocoa powder
1 teaspoon baking powder
½ teaspoon salt
¼ teaspoon xanthan gum
1 cup packed light brown sugar
½ cup granulated sugar
½ cup (1 stick) dairy-free margarine
½ cup shortening
2 eggs
1 teaspoon vanilla
1½ cups dairy-free semisweet chocolate chips
1 cup raisins
¾ cup chopped walnuts

1. Preheat oven to 350°F. Line cookies sheets with parchment paper or lightly grease and dust with flour.

2. Combine gluten-free flour, cocoa, baking powder, salt and xanthan gum in medium bowl. Beat brown sugar, granulated sugar, margarine and shortening in large bowl with electric mixer at medium speed until light and creamy. Add eggs, 1 at a time, beating well after each addition. Beat in vanilla. Add flour mixture; beat until well blended. Stir in chocolate chips, raisins and walnuts. Drop dough by tablespoonfuls onto prepared cookie sheets.

3. Bake 10 to 12 minutes or until set. Remove to wire racks to cool completely.

Makes about 4 dozen cookies

dairy-free | egg-free | nut-free

Replace the gluten-free flour blend with all-purpose flour. Replace the eggs with ½ cup of silken tofu. Omit the xanthan gum and walnuts. Proceed as directed.

sunflower cookies

dairy-free | egg-free | nut-free

1½ cups all-purpose flour
¾ teaspoon baking soda
½ teaspoon baking powder
½ teaspoon salt
½ cup shortening
½ cup sunflower seed butter
½ cup packed brown sugar
1 ripe banana
2 tablespoons granulated sugar

1. Preheat oven to 350°F. Line cookie sheets with parchment paper. Combine flour, baking soda, baking powder and salt in medium bowl.

2. Beat shortening, sunflower seed butter, brown sugar and banana in large bowl with electric mixer at medium speed until light and fluffy. Add flour mixture; beat until combined.

3. Shape dough into 1-inch balls and place 2 inches apart on cookie sheets. Place granulated sugar on shallow plate. Dip tines of fork into sugar and then press onto top of cookie twice to make crisscross design. Repeat with remaining cookies.

4. Bake 10 to 12 minutes or until light brown. Cool 2 minutes on cookie sheets. Remove to wire rack; cool completely.

Makes 2½ dozen cookies

metric conversion chart

VOLUME MEASUREMENTS (dry)

1/8 teaspoon = 0.5 mL
1/4 teaspoon = 1 mL
1/2 teaspoon = 2 mL
3/4 teaspoon = 4 mL
1 teaspoon = 5 mL
1 tablespoon = 15 mL
2 tablespoons = 30 mL
1/4 cup = 60 mL
1/3 cup = 75 mL
1/2 cup = 125 mL
2/3 cup = 150 mL
3/4 cup = 175 mL
1 cup = 250 mL
2 cups = 1 pint = 500 mL
3 cups = 750 mL
4 cups = 1 quart = 1 L

VOLUME MEASUREMENTS (fluid)

1 fluid ounce (2 tablespoons) = 30 mL
4 fluid ounces (1/2 cup) = 125 mL
8 fluid ounces (1 cup) = 250 mL
12 fluid ounces (1 1/2 cups) = 375 mL
16 fluid ounces (2 cups) = 500 mL

WEIGHTS (mass)

1/2 ounce = 15 g
1 ounce = 30 g
3 ounces = 90 g
4 ounces = 120 g
8 ounces = 225 g
10 ounces = 285 g
12 ounces = 360 g
16 ounces = 1 pound = 450 g

DIMENSIONS

1/16 inch = 2 mm
1/8 inch = 3 mm
1/4 inch = 6 mm
1/2 inch = 1.5 cm
3/4 inch = 2 cm
1 inch = 2.5 cm

OVEN TEMPERATURES

250°F = 120°C
275°F = 140°C
300°F = 150°C
325°F = 160°C
350°F = 180°C
375°F = 190°C
400°F = 200°C
425°F = 220°C
450°F = 230°C

BAKING PAN SIZES

Utensil	Size in Inches/Quarts	Metric Volume	Size in Centimeters
Baking or Cake Pan (square or rectangular)	8×8×2	2 L	20×20×5
	9×9×2	2.5 L	23×23×5
	12×8×2	3 L	30×20×5
	13×9×2	3.5 L	33×23×5
Loaf Pan	8×4×3	1.5 L	20×10×7
	9×5×3	2 L	23×13×7
Round Layer Cake Pan	8×1½	1.2 L	20×4
	9×1½	1.5 L	23×4
Pie Plate	8×1¼	750 mL	20×3
	9×1¼	1 L	23×3
Baking Dish or Casserole	1 quart	1 L	—
	1½ quart	1.5 L	—
	2 quart	2 L	—